Wisdom From the Heart

Daily Inspirations to
Support Your Life's Journey

COMPILED BY
REBECCA HALL GRUYTER
#1 INTERNATIONAL BEST SELLING AUTHOR

RHG | MEDIA PRODUCTIONS™

Wisdom from the Heart
Daily Inspirations to Support Your Life's Journey

RHG Media Productions

21519 Knoll Way, Castro Valley, CA 94546.

ISBN 978-1-7374041-6-3 (paperback)

Visit us on line at **www.YourPurposeDrivenPractice.com**

Printed in the United States of America.

ACKNOWLEDGMENTS

When writing an anthology, it takes many voices willing to join together to bring forth the book in a powerful and united way. It has been such an honor and privilege to work with this amazing group of experts who have come together with the common heartbeat of pouring into others on a daily basis. Thank you for entrusting us with your heart, wisdom and inspirations.

Thank you to my husband, who helps uplifts me with the wisdom from his heart.

Thank you to our amazing teams, communities, families, God and friends for leaning in, cheering us on and saying yes to help us bring this book forward so powerfully. It takes many hearts and spirits coming together, bringing their gifts and talents to the mix, to bring something like this book forward in multiple formats. We thank the full team, community, authors and readers for leaning in to support us in bringing this powerful book to the world. You make the journey brilliant by being on it with us.

TABLE OF CONTENTS

WISDOM FROM THE HEART

BY: REBECCA HALL GRUYTER, BOOK COMPILER

Thank you for leaning into *Wisdom From the Heart*. I'm honored and excited to bring this empowering book to you, featuring experts that are committed to helping you **listen to your heart**! Our vision is that this amazing collection of 365 inspirations will walk beside you and support you each and every day of the year, year after year. Many of us have been powerfully served by daily inspiration books, and now we are honored to have the opportunity to walk beside you and support you on a daily basis.

As an empowerment leader, I know a lot about being disempowered and how to overcome that in order to step into your passion, power and gifts so that you **shine**! The key is being willing to listen to your heart and put into action what you discover. I celebrate you saying "yes" to this book and to yourself! It is a courageous act to say "yes" to you and to be willing to let others walk beside you to support and cheer you on in life.

Life is not a solo journey, and the more we can walk beside each other and cheer each other on, the more rich and powerful our journey becomes. I believe the transformation and living a life on purpose takes place in the mindful choices we make on a day-to-day basis. And those choices add up to our week, our month and our life. This daily inspiration book is designed to support you in stopping, pausing and reflecting each day, pouring into you encouragement, truth, motivation and support into you daily.

In sharing their inspirations, our authors will equip and empower you to discover your value, align to your purpose, step forward and choose to **share the gift of you with the world.** I believe this book is a living and inter-active book that will speak wisdom, encouragement and power into your life. Your heart will be touched, and you will be motivated to take action to step forward powerfully in your life. I want to invite you to pause, take a deep breath and be ready to receive these powerful messages so they can ignite a fire in you, inspire courage in you and focus your purpose on your life to encourage you to take loving action.

We each need others to encourage us, to speak wisdom and truth into us, to love us and cheer us on and to help us stand up again when we fall. This book will walk beside you to help you run and not grow weary, to complete all that you are called to complete and to live on purpose and with great purpose.

In creating this book, I asked each heart-centered and powerful co-author to share a daily inspiration to support you, one day and one choice at a time. As they share from their respective journeys with you, they share what they have learned. They share their wisdom and what they wish someone had encouraged them with or whispered in their ear, especially in those dark and challenging times. They are committed to pouring into you and equipping and empowering you in your life. Throughout the inspirations, you will feel a consistent and transparent heartbeat to support you in very real ways as the authors often share what they wish they would have known.

We want to make your path and journey easier and purposeful for you! As the book compiler, I'm so proud of what each co-author has shared in their chapters and am honored to have each of them leaning in to support you. I am equally honored that you have said "yes" to our book and are entrusting us to support you on your journey.

Now, it's your turn. Are you going to lean in and learn from the wisdom within this book? Will you let us walk beside you on your journey of life? We want to lift you up, support you, encourage you, and empower you. It is your choice. We want to equip and empower you to take action, move forward and share your gifts with the world. You can choose to open the pages and let them pour into you, or you can put this book on a shelf. **My heart and prayer are that you will say "yes" to you and lean into the powerful messages of hope that are waiting to pour into you, your heart and your life.**

You have unique gifts, talents, abilities, stories, journeys and perspectives that you alone can bring forward. Those in your life need you, your message, your wisdom, your perspective, gifts, talents and heart. When we shrink back or hide, the world becomes less vibrant, and we all miss out. Be willing to share the gift of you with those around you and with the world! Be willing to be seen on the same level you are willing/wanting to serve.

Here is how to get the most out of this powerful book. It is divided into three sections, each one designed to meet you exactly where you are and to support you each and every day of the year. **In the first section,** you will find the daily inspiration in order of the calendar year, each month and day of the year. **In the second section,** you will find a subject section that you can look up a particular area or subject in which you want support, and it will list the inspirations that can support you in that particular area. **In the third section,** you will find all our beautiful authors' pictures, biographies and contact information. I know that they would love to hear from you and have you follow and connect with them. I encourage you to "friend" and follow those authors with whom you feel a powerful resonance and connection so that they can continue to pour into and support you on your journey in life.

Now the next step is yours. Drink in the stories and messages that are within these pages to serve, support and inspire you. Take the time to pause, read and reflect. Listen to the powerful messages of hope that are waiting for you within the pages of this book. It's not an accident that you purchased this book and are opening it to read right now today. I invite you to lean in and truly receive the messages and wisdom that will speak to your heart and soul that you will find in these transformational and dynamic pages. Enjoy this rich collection of wisdom, love and encouragement.

—Rebecca Hall Gruyter, Book Compiler

Founder/Owner of Your Purpose Driven Practice and CEO of RHG Media Productions

Rebecca Hall Gruyter is a global influencer, #1 international best-selling and award-winning author and compiler, in-demand publisher, Empowering radio show host (reaching over one million listeners on eight networks), podcast host, and an Empowerment leader who wants to help you reach more people. She has built multiple platforms to help experts reach more people. These platforms include: radio, TV, books, magazines, the Speaker Talent Search, and live events, creating a powerful promotional reach of over ten million!

Rebecca is the CEO of RHG Media Productions (which includes the RHG TV network with over thirty weekly programs and a publishing arm that has helped over 250 authors become best-sellers). She is the owner of Your Purpose Driven Practice and the creator of the Speaker Talent Search. An animal advocate and animal communicator.

RHG Media productions is an in-demand publisher that specializes in launching books as best-sellers while creating great visibility both for the author and book. She helps the author be powerfully positioned and the star of their best-selling campaign to reach as many people as possible around the world.

Rebecca has personally contributed to over thirty published books, multiple magazines and has been quoted in Major Media, *The Huffington Post*, ABC, CBS, NBC, Fox, and Thrive Global. She has been recognized as one of the top-ten working women in America by AWWIN, Inc., and now helps experts get quoted in major media, too. Today, she wants you to have impact! Be seen, heard and *shine*!

Rebecca@YourPurposeDrivenPractice.com

www.facebook.com/rhallgruyter (Facebook)

www.YourPurposeDrivenPractice.com (Main website)

www.EmpoweringWomenTransformingLives.com (Weekly radio show)

www.MeetWithRebecca.com (Calendar link to schedule a time to talk with Rebecca)

January

1.

Living On Purpose and With Purpose

Welcome to a new year of your purpose-driven life! What does this actually mean?

Your time, energy, gifts, talents and resources are precious. Choose how you are going to spend—and share—these precious gifts that make *you* who you are and how you're gifted to show up in this world. Yes, *choose*! You get to choose how to spend them on purpose and with great purpose each and every day. And when you do, you expand them and bring even more meaning to your life and to the world!

How do you do that? Here is a key practice:

- **Stop, pause and evaluate the day** before you. Look at where you are and where you want to be. Then you can make a plan to get there—for your day, your week or your month.

- **Stay intentional and mindful** as you do this, knowing you have a choice. Go through your day with this in mind: "I am making choices all day, every day, with mindfulness and purpose."

- **Choose to move forward** with those things that matter most to you.

This simple practice will create a life with more ease, productivity, action and wonderful things coming back to you. When you are living a purpose-driven life, you are doing this not just for yourself but also for those you are serving and interacting with—your employees, children, family, clients, pets, community.

Can you picture how much more strongly and easily you could show up in those places lovingly and powerfully?

Inspiration by Rebecca Hall Gruyter, Influencer, Publisher and Animal Communicator

2.

Thought for the Day

"Life happens for us, not to us."

–TONY ROBBINS

3.

New Year Bliss

"As the new year unfolds, discover the beauty of starting anew and the power of creating your own path to bliss."

–MONEEKA SAWYER, THE BLISSFUL MILLIONAIRE

As we welcome the fresh beginning of a new year, may we embrace the endless possibilities that lie ahead. Each new year presents us with a chance to start afresh, to reevaluate our goals and to pave our own paths to bliss.

Embrace the beauty of starting anew, for it is in these moments of transformation that we discover our true potential. As we shed the layers of the past, we make room for growth, creativity and joy. Make this year the year you break free from the constraints of yesterday and step boldly into a future of limitless opportunity.

Creating your own path to bliss is a powerful and empowering journey. It is about owning your choices, following your heart and living authentically. Don't be afraid to forge a path that is uniquely yours, for it is in the pursuit of your dreams that you truly find fulfillment.

As you navigate the twists and turns of the new year, remember to stay true to yourself, trust in your abilities and believe in the magic of new beginnings. May this year be filled with moments of joy, peace and endless possibilities. Here's to creating a year full of bliss and beauty.

Inspiration by Moneeka Sawyer, the Blissful Millionaire

4.

Thought for the Day

"In any given moment, we have two options: to step forward into growth or step back into safety."

–ABRAHAM MASLOW

5.

Start on Purpose

Happy New Year, friends! As we begin this fresh chapter, let's make a resolution to start the new year on purpose.

You know what I mean-no more sleepwalking through life, nodding off during the good stuff. This year, we're going to be wide awake and intentional, like a kid on Christmas morning!

Maybe your "purpose" is to deepen your faith, launch that side hustle or finally learn to bake something besides hockey pucks. (Hey, no judgment here-I once tried to make bread and ended up with a solid doorstop!)

Whatever your goal, approach it with the energy and enthusiasm of a puppy chasing a squirrel. Leap over obstacles, shake off setbacks and keep that tail wagging, with your tongue hanging out.

Because here's the thing: When we live on purpose, we open ourselves up to all the blessings God has in store. It's like leaving a trail of bread-crumbs that lead straight to His grace.

So let's make 2025 the year we stop drifting and start directing. Let's chase our dreams with wild abandon, knowing that our purposeful pursuit is pleasing to the One who dreamed us up in the first place.

Who's with me? Let's make this year one for the books or at least for your social media posts!

Inspiration by Janet Bernice Cheney, life-coach and best-selling author

6.

The Dragon's Call: Shedding Old Skin for Renewal

"The year of the dragon is revered in many cultures for its symbolism of transformation and renewal, serves as a powerful reminder of shedding old patterns and embracing growth (Wikipedia)." It's a chance to assess our journey—from where we began, where we are now and where we aspire to go. Like shedding old skin, we shed outdated energies, including people, places and things that no longer align with our energy. As Heraclitus famously said, "Change is the only constant in life," reminding us that transformation is inherent to our existence.

In embracing change, we tap into our innate power to shape our destiny. By fostering a growth mindset, authenticity and resilience, we navigate the unknown with courage and curiosity. Each transition becomes an opportunity for self-discovery and renewal, guiding us towards greater alignment with our true selves and deepest aspirations.

As we courageously embrace our own transformation, we inspire others to embark on their own journeys of growth and evolution. Together, we weave a narrative of empowerment and possibility, creating energetic positive change that reverberates far beyond ourselves.

In closing, let us remember the words of Maya Angelou, who said, "We delight in the beauty of the butterfly, but rarely admit the changes it has gone through to achieve that beauty." May we find solace in the beauty of our own transformations, embracing the journey with open hearts and steadfast determination.

Inspiration by Deborah Wiener, creator of The Energetic Business Feng Shui System™

7.

Create Your Future

Know what you want. You can't create something you can't think of, so be very clear. Imagine all the details. Write it out. Map it out. Create a vision board.

Focus less on what you don't want and more on what you do want. Start by taking a small step toward that today and then another step every day until your reach your goal.

Inspiration by Jaimie Harnagel, Shaman

8.

Take First Steps

It's important to take those first steps and trust . . . even if it is scary. You don't get anywhere if you don't take steps. One at a time and soon the next step will move you forward. Trust your heart, take steps and see the wonderful places you will go and you will see.

Inspiration by Pumpkin(g), the cat

9.

Thought for the Day

"You become what you believe."

–OPRAH WINFREY

10.

Love What You Do

"Your work is going to fill a large part of your life, and the only way to be truly satisfied is to do what you believe is great work. And the only way to do great work is to love what you do. If you haven't found it yet, keep looking. Don't settle."

−STEVE JOBS

The message resonates profoundly: passion unlocks the door to greatness. When fueled by passion, our work transforms from a mere obligation into a wellspring of joy and inspiration. This fervor propels us to transcend boundaries, innovate and shine brightly beyond the mundane. Jobs implores us to be unwavering in our quest for this passion, reminding us not to accept anything less than extraordinary.

He likens the pursuit of fulfilling work to matters of the heart, suggesting that it is a deeply personal and intuitive odyssey. Just as we recognize love upon its arrival, we will also know when we have discovered our true calling. This journey may demand patience and tenacity, yet the reward is a life infused with purpose and joy.

Ultimately, Jobs' words serve as a compelling reminder to honor our passions and seek out vocations that resonate with our innermost values and interests. By doing so, we not only achieve personal fulfillment but also make meaningful contributions to the world that surrounds us.

Inspiration by Misti Mazurik, Author and Director of Operations at RHG Media Productions

11.

Thought for the Day

"Act as if what you do makes a difference. It does."

–WILLIAM JAMES

12.

The Journey

"Maybe the journey isn't about becoming anything. Maybe it's about unbecoming everything that isn't really you, so that you can be who you were meant to be in the first place."

–PAULO COELHO

We have been molded since birth. Maybe we have to unlearn who we <u>think</u> we are or who we have become and allow ourselves to be who we were born to be.

This is your story. You are the author. You can rewrite it at any time.

Inspiration by Jaimie Harnagel, Shaman

13.

Thought for the Day

"Seventy percent of success in life is showing up."
–WOODY ALLEN

14.

We Need You to *Shine*

"What sets you apart can sometimes feel like a burden, and it's not . . . A lot of the time, it's what makes you great." -Emma Stone

You have special talents, skills and abilities unique to you. Your special combination of life experience and talent is absolutely needed in the world. No one else can bring your unique combination forward like you.

Stop.

Please read those sentences again and think about that for a moment.

You know things that no one else knows. You see things from a perspective no one else sees. You can do things no one else can do.

As a result, there are specific people you're here to serve. They need your expertise to help them with particular problems they're having. And **they need it in exactly the way you do what you do.**

This is important, *and* **this is your call to step forward.** Now, the big question is, are you willing to help the people you're here to help? It is your choice. I hope you lean in and say yes.

Inspiration by Rebecca Hall Gruyter, Influencer, Publisher and Animal Communicator

15.

Thought for the Day

"If God is your partner, make your plans BIG!"

–D.L. MOODY

16.

Connect to Others from a Place of Service

When you meet someone, and you are thinking about what you can get from them, it shows in the way you talk to them. You can cover it with the logic of how they would benefit, but your true intention always shows through, and the result is that the other person doesn't feel seen, heard or understood.

So, make sure you **cultivate the spirit of service within yourself** first.

It's perfectly fine to want something for yourself as well, but make sure you are showing up thinking *win-win*. The best way to do this is to see the world through the eyes of the person with whom you're trying to connect. Here is an exercise you can do to prepare yourself for a connection with an individual.

Sit down with a sheet of paper or screen and write out the answers to these questions from their perspective:

What are they most excited about?

What are they looking for?

What are their biggest concerns or frustrations?

What solutions are they seeking?

With this understanding, your ability to connect with them skyrockets. These are also great questions to think about before presenting to an audience. They are also great questions to explore and ask at networking events to facilitate connecting conversations coming from a place of service.

Inspiration by Rebecca Hall Gruyter, Influencer, Publisher and Animal Communicator

17.

Thought for the Day

"We accept the love we think we deserve."
—STEPHEN CHBOSKY, THE PERKS
OF BEING A WALLFLOWER

18.

How Do You Become More Visible?

You might hear from people that you need to be more visible in your business. You may believe it's a wonderful idea. But how do you start?

1. *Make a plan.*

2. *Bring in support.*

3. *Be consistent in implementing the plan.*

Your plan doesn't have to be perfect—but you must have something set down to move you forward. Your plan is the set of activities you need to do to help yourself to be seen, just like you have plans for your other goals like business sales, vacations and events. Just get started; you can shift or tweak your plan along the way.

You don't have to go it alone—life is not a solo journey. Work with a coach or mentor to develop a plan that will help you strategically build your visibility and reach your goals. Bring in support in the form of friends or team members to keep you inspired and on target.

Consistency is key. In our business and our lives, we need to make sure that we are consistent in how we show up in the world. Leaning in, then not following up, responding, then hiding or constantly shifting your plans will *not* work.

Decide to be *all in* your willingness to be visible, to *bloom* and to *shine*, and you'll be well on your way to success!

Inspiration by Rebecca Hall Gruyter, Influencer, Publisher and Animal Communicator

19.

Thought for the Day

"Life shrinks or expands in proportion to one's courage."

−ANAIS NIN

20.

What Does it Mean to "Lean In"?

For me, leaning in means **to step into what it is you are being called to do**. It means staying open to being seen, to serve and to *shine*. Yes, there will be fears, and there will be challenges, yet you are pulled by your vision to go forward, to touch the lives of others, to share and care in wondrous ways.

Former First Lady Michelle Obama shared this story in her book *Becoming*. When Barack was making the decision to run for president, Michelle felt very uncertain about this step. She had a family, a career, a life she enjoyed with her husband, and she knew all of that would change the moment he announced his candidacy. However, after deep reflection, she realized that this was what they were called to do. So, she leaned in, clearly knowing her *why*, even as she didn't yet know where this journey would take her and her family.

Leaning in means **to show up, perfect in our "imperfections."** If all of the famous leaders and influencers waited until everything was in place, every single mistake they could make was made, their future plans had all of the Ts crossed and Is dotted, I believe they would never have made any change happen at all!

Inspiration by Rebecca Hall Gruyter, Influencer, Publisher and Animal Communicator

21.

Dream Big

Your mind and heart can take you to many wonderful places. Be willing to dream big. Hold those big dreams in your heart and take those steps. Hear me cheering you on!

Inspiration by Pumpkin(g), the cat

22.

Thought for the Day

"It's not enough to have lived. We should be determined to live for something."

–WINSTON S. CHURCHILL

23.

Transform Dreams into Reality

"In the realm of new beginnings, bliss is the divine spark that ignites passion and transforms dreams into reality."

–MONEEKA SAWYER, THE BLISSFUL REBEL

Have you ever stood on the brink of something new? It's that exhilarating moment when possibilities stretch before you like a blank canvas, waiting for a passionate splash of color. And you know that magic is about to happen.

Bliss isn't just a fleeting emotion. It's the warmth that fills your heart when you follow your deepest desires. When we embark on new chapters, that divine spark propels us forward, lighting up our path even on the days when doubt creeps in. It transforms our dreams, which sometimes feel so out of reach, into solid plans fueled by love and excitement.

Imagine standing at the threshold of a fresh adventure, your spirit buzzing with the joy of possibility. When we embrace that bliss—whether it's starting a new job, moving to a new city or pursuing a new passion—we're not just chasing dreams. We're inviting a beautiful transformation.

So, as you navigate your own new beginnings, let bliss guide you. Allow it to illuminate your path and ignite the passionate fire within. After all, each new start is an opportunity to turn dreams into reality, one blissful moment at a time.

Inspiration by Moneeka Sawyer-The Blissful Rebel

24.

Thought for the Day

"To shine your brightest light is to be who you truly are."

–ROY T. BENNETT

25.

Intentional Bliss

"Happiness is not a destination, but a way of life. Live each day choosing bliss."

–MONEEKA SAWYER, THE BLISSFUL MILLIONAIRE

Today, let's shift our mindset away from constantly looking ahead to the next milestone for fulfillment. Instead, let's embrace happiness as something that can permeate every day, if we choose to live with bliss in our hearts.

This doesn't mean ignoring our goals or giving up on dreams. But it does mean learning to appreciate the journey of life, rather than obsessing about getting to the next stop. It means taking moments to feel gratitude for what we have today-the little joys and pleasures that surround us, often going unnoticed when we're intensely focused on what's next.

Living blissfully is an intentional practice of staying present, observing beauty, feeling wonder and nurturing whatever it is that sparks delight within you. It could be the warmth of a cup of coffee, the peaceful moment of meditation or the laughter of spending time with loved ones. It allows you to enjoy the entire path of life, not just await the next landmark. Yes, you may stumble, grow fatigued or weather storms at times. But walking with bliss as your steady companion, you can move fluidly, curiosity ever-alive.

Choose to focus on bliss? Choosing bliss will free you from constantly striving to get somewhere else, untethering happiness from the unknown future. It shows you that your journey, in its richness and totality, offers boundless chances to feel alive each and every day.

Inspiration by Moneeka Sawyer, the Blissful Millionaire

26.

Thought for the Day

"Let your Spirit lead you and your light will shine ever bright."

–LESLIE C. DOBSON, YOU WERE MADE TO SHINE

27.

What Are You Choosing to Entertain?

Every day, we receive thousands of messages, information, opportunities—some based on positivity and hope, some based on fear and scarcity. With so much input and such busy lives to lead, it can become easy to just allow it all in and move forward the best we can.

Here is what happens: the fear and scarcity creep in slowly and sometimes quietly until you find that you are moving away from your dreams and purpose instead of toward what it is that you want.

It becomes time to draw the line for yourself—what are you choosing to entertain? For me, the inner conversation is to contemplate these questions:

Is this thing meaningful and serving my purpose and my values?

Am I moving forward with ease and positivity?

If any of these answers are no, then I choose to stand my ground and not entertain the opposite of the energy that serves me. **I choose not to hold court for the worry and other negative possibilities.**

Isn't that powerful and purposeful? Yes, it is!

As I'm watching what's happening worldwide and in our country, I am looking for the good, the loving and the positive that I can entertain. I'm looking for what we can unite around and claim, to bring forward for health and healing and vibrancy and collaboration.

What are the positive things that you can see in the world? *Into what are you choosing to put your energy?*

Inspiration by Rebecca Hall Gruyter, Influencer, Publisher and Animal Communicator

28.

Stop. Pause. Listen. Then Choose.

I believe the ability to live on purpose and with purpose is tied closely to stopping, pausing and listening. June is the perfect month to pause, sit in your garden or yard or a field with a nice cold beverage, shoes kicked off and legs outstretched. Ah!

Feel the breeze, smell the flowers and listen to the buzz of the flies, tree frogs and locusts. And listen within. Living a life on purpose and with purpose means listening for the wisdom your heart has to tell you. Take a deep breath and lean in a little more to the reminder of who you are and what you are called to bring forth.

Then choose your next steps on purpose and in alignment with what matters most to you to bring forward, one breath, step and choice at a time.

Inspiration by Rebecca Hall Gruyter, Influencer, Publisher and Animal Communicator

29.

Thought for the Day

"One is loved because one is loved. No reason is needed for loving."

–PAULO COELHO, THE ALCHEMIST

30.

Thought for the Day

*"I can't change the world but I can
change the world in me."*

–BONO

31.

You Are a Wonder!

*"You are a wonder! We stand in awe of all
you are, are becoming and will be."*

Inspiration by The Georgies, cat, from the Book Collective

February

1.

Spring Forward and *Shine*!

"You can have roots and wings."

-JAKE, IN SWEET HOME ALABAMA

There's something about a seed knowing what it is and what it's going to become. It starts digging its roots in deep so that it can grow and shine as it's made to do. That describes us as well! We can lean into who we truly are, what we truly need and who we are truly made to be. Sometimes it's hidden deep down under old stories and messages we've received, but we are gifted to serve with all our unique talents, abilities and dreams, just like the rose has been gifted with color, scent, delicate petals and strong stems.

I believe you "can have roots and wings," as Jake says in the movie *Sweet Home Alabama.* **In fact, we** *need* **both to shine.** We have roots that we send down deep into the earth, a foundation for the actions that will support us in bringing forward what we are called to do and be. Our roots are our plans, our talents, our resources and the loving people who support us. Our deep roots help us weather the storms of life as we grow and blossom.

We also have wings—dreams, goals, callings—that pull us to fly! Our wings take us to new opportunities to *shine* and to light the path for others. We're able to spring forward to *shine* because we have our roots to support us.

Today, let's celebrate our roots and our wings and all the gifts we've been given to share! **Let your roots go deep, and your wings give flight to your dreams, passion and purpose.**

Inspiration by Rebecca Hall Gruyter, Influencer, Publisher and Animal Communicator

2.

Thought for the Day

"The earth is gentle. And the earth allows the flowers to bloom. We need to be gentle. And the flowers will bloom in our life."

–AVIJEET DAS

3.

Thought for the Day

"A friend is a gift you give yourself."
–ROBERT LOUIS STEVENSON

4.

You Deserve Love

"You yourself, as much as anybody in the entire universe, deserve your love and affection."

–BUDDHA

This profound quote by Buddha emphasizes the importance of self-love and self-compassion. In a world that often prioritizes external achievements and validations, it is easy to neglect our own emotional and spiritual well-being. Buddha's words remind us that we are deserving of the same kindness and affection that we readily offer to others. This self-love is not about being self-centered or narcissistic but about recognizing our own worth and treating ourselves with the same respect and care that we extend to our loved ones.

When we practice self-love, we build a solid foundation for our mental and emotional health. It allows us to set healthy boundaries, make better decisions and cultivate a sense of inner peace. Furthermore, self-love is essential for personal growth and resilience, helping us to navigate life's challenges with grace and strength. It fosters a positive self-image and enhances our capacity for empathy and compassion towards others.

Moreover, self-love is a journey that requires ongoing effort and mindfulness. It involves acknowledging our flaws and imperfections, forgiving ourselves for past mistakes and celebrating our achievements, no matter how small. By embracing Buddha's wisdom, we can learn to nurture ourselves and create a more balanced and fulfilling life. After all, when we love and care for ourselves, we are better equipped to spread love and compassion to those around us, contributing to a more harmonious and compassionate world.

Inspiration by Misti Mazurik, Author and Director of Operations at RHG Media Productions

5.

Thought for the Day

"You came to RADIATE the fullness of who you are."

−ABRAHAM HICKS

6.

Alignment

"True Bliss is when what you do, say, and think are all aligned."

–MONEEKA SAWYER, THE BLISSFUL MILLIONAIRE

Living a life that is true to yourself means embodying authenticity in all aspects of your being. Being honest with yourself and others, and staying true to your values and beliefs. When what you do, say and think are all aligned, you are living in integrity with who you truly are.

It is easy to get caught up in the expectations and judgments of others, but true bliss comes when you listen to the whisper of your own heart and follow its guidance. Trusting yourself and staying true to your inner voice will lead you on a path of abundance and joy.

Being aligned in your actions, words, and thoughts requires self-awareness and reflection. Take the time to tune in to your thoughts and feelings, and make conscious choices that align with your truest self. Set intentions that are in line with your deepest desires and dreams, and watch as your life transforms into a beautiful symphony of alignment.

Remember, true bliss is not about achieving perfection but about progress and growth. Today, slow down enough to embrace the journey of aligning your actions, words and thoughts, and allow yourself the grace to learn along the way. When you commit to living in alignment with your true self, you will discover a profound sense of joy, peace and fulfillment that radiates from within.

Inspiration by Moneeka Sawyer, the Blissful Millionaire

7.

Thought for the Day

"Constant kindness can accomplish much. As the sun makes ice melt, kindness causes misunderstanding, mistrust, and hostility to evaporate."

–ALBERT SCHWEITZER

8.

Are You Hiding Your Light?

"The only one keeping us a best-kept secret is ourselves, and the only one who can share it is ourselves."

-REBECCA HALL GRUYTER

When I talk to people about their business and their message, so many of them tell me that they want to make a positive difference. I notice that while they truly want to make a powerful difference in the world, many don't know how to go about making that happen. These beautiful, generous, gifted people are the best-kept secret, defined as *something very good that not many people know about*. They are hiding their light that they could be *shining* out into the world.

Perhaps you, too, want to make a positive difference, to impact people in a powerful, transformative way. **Do people know that about you? Do they know how to find you? Are you hiding your light?**

I have discovered that if the people who need you cannot see you and hear you, then you cannot help them. This is why I believe visibility is so important. Visibility is about being seen in such a way that you are easy for people to find.

Too many of us are waiting on the sidelines to be discovered! But the truth is: No one can make your dreams come true except you—your positive impact is not going to happen by keeping it a secret. **If you want to make a difference, you have to lead your own effort.** Become a spokesperson for your message, your product launch, your book, standing for what you believe and bringing that forward rather than merely hoping it will speak for itself. If your visibility is low, then it's up to you to raise it—no one else can do it better than you can!

Inspiration by Rebecca Hall Gruyter, Influencer, Publisher and Animal Communicator

9.

Safe to Love

Oh . . . I love love. I work with people in their hearts where love lives. Sometimes hearts are locked away in fear . . . people hide them and I have to sneak into their heart and remind them that they are safe. It is safe. You are safe. Remind your heart that it is safe and so are you. It is safe to love and be loved.

Inspiration by Pumpkin(g), the cat

10.

Thought for the Day

"It's not the people in our lives who make our lives, but loving them does."

–ANONYMOUS, HALLMARK CHANNEL

11.

Your Heart Knows

Listen to your heart and follow it. Trust it.

What is it saying to you today?

Inspiration by Jaimie Harnagel, Shaman

12.

Thought for the Day

"To fall in love with yourself is the first secret to happiness."

–ROBERT MORLEY

13.

Thought for the Day

"Let all that you do be done in love."
–1 CORINTHIANS 16:14 (ESV)

14.

Thought for the Day

"Let us always meet each other with smile,
for the smile is the beginning of love."

–MOTHER THERESA

15.

Blissful Love

"Love is the natural consequence of allowing bliss to bloom in every aspect of your life."

−MONEEKA SAWYER, THE BLISSFUL MILLIONAIRE

Love is often seen as something that just happens to you, but what if I told you that love is actually a choice that you make every day? It's true-when you allow bliss to thrive in every corner of your life, love has no choice but to follow.

Imagine waking up each day with a heart full of gratitude, a mind filled with positivity and a spirit brimming with joy. That's the power of allowing bliss to bloom. When you choose to see the beauty in everyday moments, to appreciate the little things and to spread kindness wherever you go, love naturally flows in and around you.

Whether it's the love you have for yourself, for others or for life itself, it all starts with allowing bliss to take root in your heart. Embrace the moments that bring you joy, let go of negativity and watch as love blossoms in ways you never thought possible.

Remember, love is not just a feeling-it's a choice. So today, choose to allow bliss to bloom in every aspect of your life. Every time you notice an opportunity to feel bliss, note it down. Write down, "I am blissful for/because/about . . ." And let love be the natural consequence of that decision. Trust me, the world will be a more beautiful place because of it.

Inspiration by Moneeka Sawyer, the Blissful Millionaire

16.

Thought for the Day

"When one door of happiness closes, another opens; but often we look so long at the closed door that we do not see the one which has been opened for us."

–HELEN KELLER

17.

Thought for the Day

"Forget about the fast lane. If you really want to fly, just harness your power to your passion."

–OPRAH WINFREY

18.

Keep Your Focus

I know, I know . . . February is the month when New Year's resolutions–dump that–I call them goals–start looking mighty tempting to abandon. I mean, who's idea was that anyway!! The dog needs walking, you need to go out with friends or give your companion more one-on-one time. The couch is calling, the snacks are beckoning and suddenly, that big dream feels like more work than it's worth. But you know what?

You can treat yourself to a serving of commitment, with a hefty side of grace for the days you stumble. This is your month to shine!

I'm taking a page from the gospel of Treat Yo'Self and making focus my new obsession this month. Because here's the truth: Nothing worth having comes easy, but it's oh-so-worth-it in the end!

So, when you feel that motivation starting to waver, remember **why** you started. Was it to honor God with your gifts? To set an example for your loved ones? To finally pursue that long-simmering passion?

Whatever your "why," let it be your focus-snack. Take a little bite whenever you need to re-energize your drive. And while you're at it, maybe grab an actual snack too; I find that Thin Mints pair exceptionally well with determined perseverance. (And there are even some that are gluten-free!)

Inspiration by Janet Bernice Cheney, life-coach and best-selling author

19.

Harnessing Intuition Through Body Awareness

Let me take you back to when I was ten years old, bullied into barreling down a steep snowy hill on a rusty old makeshift sled by my "friends?" where I suffered multiple traumatic physical and emotional injuries. In that moment, fear overpowered my ability to listen to my gut feeling to protect myself. If I could speak to my younger self, I would tell her, 'Don't listen to them, listen to how you feel! Listen to your body. Say NO! No is a complete sentence.'

Practice checking in with your body's signals. Pause and notice how different situations, people and places make you feel physically. Your body often signals when something is off or not aligned with your truth. Get to know your body's signals; build a relationship with your own built-in perfectly attuned GPS system. My body communicates through my stomach and my heart. A stomachache and anxiety are a no, excitement in my heart is a yes. Your body may send you signals through a headache, pain or other uncomfortable sensations.

I encourage you to embrace the practice of body awareness as a sacred ritual. When we tune in with an open heart to our intuition and listen to the whispers of our body, we tap into a wellspring of wisdom that guides us towards our truth. Remember, your intuition is your greatest ally, ready to illuminate the path ahead if only you pause, listen and trust. It will never point you in the wrong direction.

Inspiration by Deborah Wiener, creator of The Energetic Business Feng Shui System™

20.

Messages of the Heart

There are so many messages and beings that are coming together just for you! You are so loved and supported...though you may not always recognize the love and support around you. What animal, insect, bug, bird, creature has caught your eye, heart or spirit today? In your dreams or around you on your daily journey? Take a moment to pause and ask: What message do you have for me today? And listen to the answers. Look up the meaning/symbolism of that animal/creature and see what message you discover on line that resonates with your heart?

Love is all around you. Remember to stop and listen to the loving messages and their messengers. They have been exquisitely chosen to connect with you and encourage/support you on your journey.

Inspiration by The Animal Council, from The Book Collective

21.

Kindness and Love

"Rebellion, when draped in bliss , becomes a balm rather than a blade; choose transformation that caresses the heart and speaks eloquently in the language of love."

–MONEEKA SAWYER, THE BLISSFUL REBEL

We live in a world where rebellion is often depicted as loud, aggressive and forceful. However, this quote beautifully reminds us that there's a different way to express our dissent—one that takes root in gentleness and compassion. Imagine rebellion not as a blade that cuts but as a soothing balm that heals.

When we choose to challenge societal norms or injustices, why not do so through acts of kindness and love? Picture the profound impact of transformations that prioritize understanding and empathy. A blissful rebellion is one that caresses the heart, resonating deeply rather than driving a wedge.

So, let's reframe how we engage with the world around us. In a time where tension often prevails, let us choose a path of transformation that draws us all closer, that uplifts rather than tears down. As we challenge the status quo, let's remember that gentle rebellion holds the power to transform hearts and minds, effectively creating a ripple of love. When we act with kindness, our message becomes one that lingers beautifully—the language of love spoken fluently.

What kindness can you share today that will uplift someone's life, and create a beautiful connection of love and joy? Any simple gesture—a listening ear, a warm hug or words of encouragement—can shift perspectives and inspire change.

Inspiration by Moneeka Sawyer-The Blissful Rebel

22.

Thought for the Day

"If God is your partner, make your plans BIG!"

–D.L. MOODY

23.

Thought for the Day

"Definiteness of purpose is the starting point of all achievement."

–W. CLEMENT STONE

24.

Nothing But Love

As babies, we are born with love in our hearts. We all need love. We all seek it. Sometimes from whatever source we can get it because it is a driving force.

We love our animals; they in turn love us. We care for our plants, nurturing them.

Everything is love. Love is everything.

Spend less time judging and spend more time loving.

We are all One.

Inspiration by Jaimie Harnagel, Shaman

25.

Thought for the Day

"When we love, we always strive to become better than we are. When we strive to become better than we are, everything around us becomes better too."

–PAULO COELHO, THE ALCHEMIST

26.

Grounded in Your Truth as You Fly

"Flying starts from the ground. The more grounded you are, the higher you fly."

−J.R. RIM

I believe it's important in all things that we do to stay grounded in our truth, our *why*. This is the key to living on purpose, blooming, shining and soaring. We need to take the time to truly discover our *why*—our motivation and purpose. Once we gain clarity on our purpose, we are then able to know more easily what to say *yes* to and what to say *no* to.

We say *yes* to the things that matter most to us and to the things that will help us move forward. And then, we can confidently say *no* to the things that we know will move us further away from our purpose.

This keeps us grounded in our roots and in our truth and helps us *bloom*, to move forward into doing things that keep us more fully being all that we are called and created to be and to become. Our purpose will motivate us to take action even when we hit challenges. We now begin to *shine* in alignment with our truth and spread our light outward into the world. Then, the only way to go is up, to *soar!*

Inspiration by Rebecca Hall Gruyter, Influencer, Publisher and Animal Communicator

27.

Thought for the Day

"Where there is love there is life."

–MAHATMA GANDHI

28.

Is this a Yes?

When I say *yes* to something, I know I'm saying *no* to something else I may not even know about yet.

Think about that for a moment. This means that with each opportunity that comes my way, I really want to make sure that **it is the way I am called to serve at the highest level.**

Remember, when you say yes to something, you are saying no to other things. So, take a moment to stop, pause and feel. Is this truly a yes for you, or are you getting caught up in a moment of excitement or the "shoulds"? Truly feel into *what* you are called to do and bring forward. Is this an opportunity that is truly a "yes" for you? **We can serve our whole lives in important, fulfilling ways without trying to fit ourselves into an opportunity that isn't in alignment with who we are, who we want to be or what we value.**

Is the opportunity you are considering truly a "yes" for you?

Inspiration by Rebecca Hall Gruyter, Influencer, Publisher and Animal Communicator

March

1.

Just As You Are

What can hold us back from being *blooming* and *shining* can be our own assumptions about the value of our qualities. We can ask ourselves: *What do I possibly have to contribute? I'm too shy to be a speaker. For people to respect me, I have to be [shorter, taller, thinner, heavier, better dressed, more eloquent]!*

Have you ever had statements like these looping in your brain?

For a long time, I hid my laugh because I was told it wasn't professional, so I *assumed* that it was a terrible quality for a serious businesswoman/ speaker/leader. Then a coach told me that it was part of who I am and to embrace it. I felt empowered to lean in, even to this part of me, and what did I find? People leaned into me even closer and laughed with me! In fact, that was what they remembered and loved about me, and it always made them smile.

Be willing to be seen and heard, to be visible—just as you are.

Sometimes the journey to being visible can be uncomfortable and make you feel vulnerable. But think about this: What if by doing that uncomfortable, difficult, scary thing, you made a difference for another person? Or maybe hundreds or thousands of people? That is your potential power of showing up and leaning in. Share your gifts, your uniqueness, your "you-ness."

Inspiration by Rebecca Hall Gruyter, Influencer, Publisher and Animal Communicator

2.

Do you truly see?

I am a stick bug and you won't really see me unless you look really closely. This is true for you too. You are more than you let people know. You are more than what they see at first glance... maybe even more than you let yourself see too.

Be willing to look deeply and share fully. This you see, is how you can have the impact you long to have. Be seen deeply and share your light fully.

Inspiration by Twiggy, the Stick Bug, from The Book Collective

3.

Thought for the Day

"Success is getting what you want,
happiness is wanting what you get."

–INGRID BERGMAN

4.

Thought for the Day

"Fail faster, succeed sooner."

–DR. CHERYL LENTZ

5.

Send Out Ripples of Light and *Shine*!

"Step out of hiding onto the center stage of your life."

-REBECCA HALL GRUYTER

The calling of my heart is to help others know how valuable, gifted and wonderfully made they are—and that means you! This is because I know, deeply, that you are a light that can shine so brightly that it can be seen even in the darkness. You can be the light of hope and encouragement for another! Whether it's in your business, volunteer work, relationships or strangers, you can send out rippling rays of light wherever you are.

Inspiration by Rebecca Hall Gruyter, Influencer, Publisher and Animal Communicator

6.

Thought for the Day

"Don't be pushed around by the fears in your mind. Be led by the dreams in your heart."

–ROY T. BENNETT, THE LIGHT IN THE HEART

7.

Thought for the Day

"It takes courage to not only accept our limitations but embrace our potential."

–ERWIN RAPHAEL MCMANUS

8.

Happy Women's Empowerment Day

"Women with power can bring a compassionate revolution. My mother first gave me the gift of a woman's compassion. Now, the next generation of women must bring this compassion into positions of power."

–HIS HOLINESS THE DALAI LAMA

Happy International Woman's Day! I love this quote by His Holiness the Dalai Lama for so many reasons. But most of all it's because it reminds us as women of what we are capable of. As women, we are becoming more and more powerful in society. We are more recognized for our talents and are climbing to higher positions of power. It's an amazing thing. It's also an amazing responsibility.

Remember as a woman to bring your feminine qualities wherever you go, wherever you lead. The world needs more of the feminine. Empower that part of yourself, stand in that power and lead with your natural gifts.

As His Holiness the Dalai Lama said so eloquently, one of our biggest gifts we bring as women into everything we do is compassion. It's not our only gift, but it is the gift we can share no matter who we are with, where we are or what we are doing. So today, commit to choosing compassion in every circumstance you encounter. Repeat all day, "Today I choose compassion" to keep it front of mind. Allow yourself to be a beacon of love and bliss. Share your strength and empower those around you to do the same.

Inspiration by Moneeka Sawyer, the Blissful Millionaire

9.

Thought for the Day

"A friend is one that knows you as you are,
understands where you have been, accepts what you
have become, and still, gently allows you to grow."

–WILLIAM SHAKESPEARE

10.

Thought for the Day

"I never dreamed about success. I worked for it."

–ESTEE LAUDER

11.

Thought for the Day

"The most common way people give up their power is by thinking they don't have any."

–ALICE WALKER

12.

Calling all Sheroes-Women's Empowerment Month!

So, listen up! March is our month to celebrate the unstoppable force of women, Sheroes, as a dear friend refers to us . . . sister/friends. We are brave, brilliant and basically superheroes without the capes (though I do love an eternal red scarf).

This month, I challenge you to embrace your inner Sheroe and slay every single day. Strut into that boardroom with your "I was born for this" attitude fully engaged. Ask for that raise or promotion; you've more than earned it with your talent and tenacity. And if anyone dares to question you? Give 'em your signature "you didn't just say that, did you?" stare and keep moving, sis.

Because here's the truth, straight from one who knows: We are enough, just the way we are right now, scars, mistakes and all . . . *more than enough*, actually. We didn't stumble into this world. We're here to learn, progress, overcome and heal. Then we rise!

You know the saying: "But what if I fall?" But oh, my darling, what if you fly?!

Just remember, your worth isn't measured by others' opinions or society's expectations. It's an intrinsic, God-given radiance that shines from within, illuminating all you touch.

So, let's spend March flooding the world with light, shall we? Lift up a fellow Shero, share your hard-won wisdom and bask in the glory of your own unique brilliance. This is your time to reign!

Inspiration by Janet Bernice Cheney, life-coach and best-selling author

13.

Happiness

"When I was five years old, my mother always told me that happiness was the key to life. When I went to school, they asked me what I wanted to be when I grew up. I wrote down 'happy.' They told me I didn't understand the assignment, and I told them they didn't understand life." – John Lennon

John Lennon's poignant reflection resonates deeply with me, revealing the simplicity and profundity of true wisdom. At its essence, this quote encapsulates the innocent clarity of a child's viewpoint, effortlessly slicing through the intricate web of societal expectations and norms. Lennon's mother bestowed a timeless truth: that happiness reigns as the ultimate pursuit in life. Though seemingly straightforward, this notion challenges the conventional yardsticks of success—wealth, status and career milestones.

This quote beckons us to reassess our priorities, urging that the ultimate aim of all our pursuits should revolve around achieving happiness. It invites us to embrace a more holistic definition of success, one that cherishes inner joy and contentment as fervently, if not more so, than external accolades. In a world frequently propelled by competition and materialism, Lennon's wisdom offers a refreshing and vital reminder to seek fulfillment in the simplest yet most profound treasures of existence. What makes you happy?

Inspiration by Misti Mazurik, Author and Director of Operations at RHG Media Productions

14.

Thought for the Day

"I'm a success today because I had a friend who believed in me and I didn't have the heart to let him down."

–ABRAHAM LINCOLN

15.

The Magic of Animals

Animals are here to support us and guide us. We just need to listen so we can hear what they are trying to teach us. Don't let the exterior fool you. Even the smallest animal or insect can have a great impact. They can teach us so much about ourselves and our purpose here on Earth.

If you feel connected with or drawn to animals, whether in body or spirit, you can communicate with them. If you are not sure how, you can take a basic animal communication class and reconnect with your past furry friends, talk with your current pets or even animals in nature.

There is magic in this, and you would be surprised at what animals can reveal, not just about day-to-day things but about life on a bigger scale, your purpose, their mission in being with you, past lives, everything!

There is magic all around you. Be open to seeing it.

Inspiration by Jaimie Harnagel, Shaman

16.

Mastering Destiny: The Transformative Power of Stoic Philosophy

Very little is needed to make a happy life; it is all within yourself and in your way of thinking. I define Stoicism as an ancient philosophy grounded in logic and practicality; it offers a transformative approach to life and healing. At its core, Stoicism instills a sense of accountability, reminding us that we are the masters of our own fate and that there are no victims in Stoicism—only individuals empowered to shape their destinies.

Stoicism is both an intellectual and spiritual practice, guiding us to navigate life's challenges with wisdom, grace and equanimity. It encourages us to confront adversity head-on, reframing our perspective to see obstacles as opportunities for growth and transformation.

By embracing stoic principles, we become more self-reflective, cultivating a heightened awareness of our thoughts, emotions and actions. Self-awareness fosters personal growth and resilience, allowing us to live and function at a higher vibration and frequency. By taking ownership and becoming aware of our thoughts and actions, we harness the power of the law of attraction, attracting positivity and abundance into our lives.

In the words of Marcus Aurelius, "The happiness of your life depends upon the quality of your thoughts: therefore, guard accordingly . . . You have power over your mind-not outside events. Realize this, and you will find strength." Let us heed these words and embrace the wisdom of Stoicism as we journey towards conscious evolution.

Inspiration by Deborah Wiener, creator of The Energetic Business Feng Shui System™

17.

Thought for the Day

*"There is no greater agony than bearing
an untold story inside you."*

–MAYA ANGELOU, KNOW WHY THE CAGED BIRD SINGS

18.

Seeds

Dear one, feel me coming along side you, joining you, and partnering with you. What can and will we create together I lean in and ask you. What seeds are you planting that I may help and support you in their growth?

Invite me in to bring my wisdom, nurturing and power to grow your seeds mightily. I am waiting for you...the soil/ground is ready....let's plant seeds to bear the fruit you are seeking in your life.

Inspiration by Gaia, Mother Earth, from The Book Collective

19.

Thought for the Day

"Patience, persistence and perspiration make an unbeatable combination for success."

–NAPOLEON HILL

20.

Bliss Revolution

"In the quiet stirrings of the heart lies the power to change the world—let your bliss revolution begin within."

–MONEEKA SAWYER, THE BLISSFUL REBEL

Have you ever paused amidst the chaos of life and felt that subtle spark in your heart? It whispers, urging you to consider the world around you and your very place in it. This quote beautifully reminds us that change doesn't always need to be loud or grand; sometimes, it begins with softly nurturing our inner landscapes.

Imagine if everyone let their personal revolutions blossom. How transformative would our communities, our relationships, our workplaces become if each of us took the time to cultivate kindness and empathy within? Often, we assume great change is only reserved for those in positions of power, but it starts with us. The daily choices we make—offering a smile, listening attentively or just being present for someone—can set off ripples that reach far beyond our immediate circle.

Let today be the day we honor those quiet stirrings within us. It could be as simple as a moment of gratitude or a tiny act of compassion. With every blissful choice we make, we collectively weave a more loving world. Remember, the journey of a thousand miles begins with a single, heartfelt step. Are you ready to let your bliss revolution begin?

Inspiration By Moneeka Sawyer-The Blissful Rebel

21.

Thought for the Day

"Act as if it was, and it will be."
–LAILAH GIFTY AKITA, PEARLS OF WISDOM: GREAT MIND

22.

Thought for the Day

"It's not whether you get knocked down. It's whether you get up."

–VINCE LOMBARD

23.

Thought for the Day

"Shine like a rising Sun."

–LAILAH GIFTY AKITA

24.

Winter Always Turns to Spring

Grief. What I have learned is we process grief on four different levels: Emotional, Physical, Mental and Spiritual.

We go through the range of emotions that come with loss . . . shock, disbelief, denial, sadness, etc. This is normal for us humans.

We experience the loss of the physical, not being able to see, touch, hear the loved one's voice.

We try to rationalize or understand the loss . . . how could this have happened? Who is to blame? What caused it? Why?

But if we step back and look at the bigger picture, we can see that they did what they came here to do and perhaps their journey was complete. We are the ones that are grieving, but they are ready for the next beautiful new beginning. Because after all, death is a rebirth.

Remember to look for the gifts that our loved ones leave us with, and remember too, that no matter how long and dark a winter is, it always turns into spring.

Inspiration by Jaimie Harnagel, Shaman

25.

Chase the Rainbows

Color therapy is an easy tool to bring into the mix. We already do it throughout the day in many ways.

You actually know exactly what color you need. For example, look at what clothes you reach for in the morning. What color are you drawn to? What are you in the mood for? What is the vibration? Red has a different vibration than blue or purple. How does yellow feel? Etc.

What colors do you choose to surround yourself with? Do they lift you up and energize you? Calm you?

You can make even more conscious choices so that you can get more out of your day.

Every color has a vibration.

What color are you today? What energy do you want to bring in? Allow colors to come in and support you.

Be purposeful when you choose the color for the day. Pick the colors that make you feel joyful and supportive of you.

Inspiration by Jaimie Harnagel, Shaman

26.

Thought for the Day

"Authenticity is a collection of choices that we have to make every day... The choice to let ourselves be seen."

–DR. BRENE BROWN

27.

Home

When I was an outside cat looking for a home, I was told "No" a lot. Doors were shut in my face, hurtful words were thrown at me . . . it was hard, scary and lonely. Then I found my mom and I felt her love beam out at me, calling me home. I had to be courageous and persistent. I let her know I had chosen her and wouldn't leave until she gave me a home. I never gave up and I kept showing up.

I found my home and family. You too can find your home, your place. Keep showing up, stand your ground and reach out from your heart. You too will find where you belong.

Inspiration by Pumpkin(g), the cat

28.

Thought for the Day

"I want to get you excited about who you are, what you are, what you have, and what can still be for you. I want to inspire you to see that you can go far beyond where you are right now."

–VIRGINIA SATIR

29.

Thought for the Day

"Flying starts from the ground. The more grounded you are, the higher you fly."

–J.R. RIM

30.

Walk Through Your Fear

To support us in stepping through our fear, I find tapping into our "why" to be powerfully motivating when I face my fear. Here are the steps I go through to walk through it.

1. **Stop. Pause. Explore what I'm afraid of.**

2. **Feel the feeling,** but then explore why it's important to me that I step through it, that I don't let the feeling of fear stop me.

3. **How can I set myself up for success in this situation?** What can I do to help me feel safer and supported as I step into this new space? Is it getting support? Is it giving myself permission to leave if I need to?

4. **ake action and lean in and step forward**—even if it's a first small step.

I find every time I survive stepping into a new level, my muscle grows stronger, I gain more strength and eventually, I'm able to soar in that space—and then discover another level that can be stepped into!

Each step prepares you for the next, and you get to build the muscles and strength more visibly on the journey, one step at a time. What step can you take today?

Inspiration by Rebecca Hall Gruyter, Influencer, Publisher and Animal Communicator

31.

Thought for the Day

"Power is not given to you. You have to take it."
−BEYONCE KNOWLES

April

1.

Choose to Share the Gift of You with the World

"Insanity: doing the same thing over and over again and expecting different results." -Unknown

The world is waiting for the gift of more of you! I know you are sharing what you're called forth to bring to the world in your life and business. And I encourage and support you to share even more of you!

Let's check in on how you're doing: What actions are you taking that you'll be practicing or implementing that are different from last year (further expanding and helping you grow), and will bring you different results that you want?

Often, we can be doing the same things—just pushing harder—and be expecting different results. You have choices in everything that you're doing and can make different choices that better serve you. Think about what you can choose to echo out, the things that will allow you to be seen and heard, even more, to be visible!

Visibility is how you are showing up in the world. It could be on stage, on the radio or on the grocery line! I believe so much that **visibility is how you best share the gift of yourself with the world.**

Today, think about how you are showing up in your life for yourself and for others. **You are called to be visible, to show up exactly as you are made.** Be willing to build new practices and take new actions today that might be different from what you did last year so that you can be even more visible or in a different way that lets you *shine* even brighter.

Inspiration by Rebecca Hall Gruyter, Influencer, Publisher and Animal Communicator

2.

Thought for the Day

"The tiny seed knew that in order to grow, it needed to be dropped in dirt, covered with darkness, and struggle to reach the light."

–SANDRA KRING

3.

Thought for the Day

*"Don't be afraid to speak up for yourself.
Keep fighting for your dreams!"*

–GABBY DOUGLAS

4.

Choose to Shine

"The more you shine, *the more you are paving the way for others."*
-Rebecca Hall Gruyter

I'm passionate about empowering women and men because I know firsthand what it's like to come from a much-disempowered place. I experienced all types of abuse during my most formative years. This environment of abuse made me believe false messages like I am not okay, there is something wrong with me and that it is *not* safe to be seen or heard.

As a result, I became an expert in hiding. When I was finally rescued, I was able to start my healing journey. I discovered that these beliefs I had embraced all those years were actually lies. **I discovered that I am beautifully and wonderfully made, and so are you! I discovered that I matter and am needed just as I am—and that it is safe to be seen, heard and shine. The same is true for you too!**

It became my mission (and it still is!) to help others understand these same truths. My life and work have taken me to places I could never have dreamed of, reaching thousands of people all over the world with my message because I have chosen to *shine.*

When you share the amazing gift of *you,* the more you shine, and the more you pave the way for others to shine too! How can you share more of yourself and *shine* (share) the fit of you with the world?

Inspiration by Rebecca Hall Gruyter, Influencer, Publisher and Animal Communicator

5.

Thought for the Day

"Be patient with yourself. Self-growth is tender; it's holy ground. There's no greater investment."

–STEPHEN COVEY

6.

What Lights You Up?

Think of everyday things that support and lift you up. Even if you dread your job, find one thing every day that brings you joy. Find little things to lift your spirit. Eat lunch outside, reach out to people that lift you up, take fifteen minutes for yourself to do something you love.

What lights you up? Pursue that. Take a step towards that. Start with a few minutes a day. Get the ball rolling until it becomes a snowball!

Don't let fear keep you from doing what you want to do.

Say YES to what you truly love.

Inspiration by Jaimie Harnagel, Shaman

7.

Thought for the Day

"Finish each day be done with it. You have done what you could. Some blunders and absurdities no doubt crept in; forget them as soon as you can. Tomorrow is a new day. You shall begin it serenely and with too high a spirit to be encumbered with your old nonsense."

–RALPH WALDO EMERSON

8.

"Who's Ready to Reach the World?"

Several years ago, I found myself saying yes to an opportunity to create an online TV channel with VoiceAmerica. I knew almost nothing about what I was getting into; the project stood in front of me, ready to manifest. In a few days, I was going to host one of my live Women's Empowerment daylong events.

I stood on the stage of the event to give my talk, and something came to me that was so miraculous. Something that I would not have even thought of thinking! It was such a God thing at that moment. It came to me to share the project and announce to the audience, **"So, who will join me? Who's ready to reach the world and be on this journey with me? I don't know where it'll go, but I know it's not just for me. It's for all of you! Who's with me?"**

I paused, wondering what I had just done. To my delight, people stood up and got on that stage! It was an amazing moment of excitement, possibility and love. Some did sign up that day, as well as others later. We launched it as scheduled, and within just a few months, it became the number-one, most-watched channel.

My lessons are these: **You don't always know how your yes is going to be accomplished. You don't have to do it alone. And it's always about something bigger than yourself. Who can you invite to join you on your journey?**

Inspiration by Rebecca Hall Gruyter, Influencer, Publisher and Animal Communicator

9.

Thought for the Day

"Guess what? You're in charge! Don't let the day tell you otherwise."

–REBECCA HALL GRUYTER

10.

Thought for the Day

"Stop limiting your potential. Realize that there's an unlimited amount of things that you can do with your life."

–SONYA PARKER

11.

Thought for the Day

"Efforts and courage are not enough without purpose and direction."

–JOHN F. KENNEDY

12.

Making Empowered Choices

"Every problem is a gift—without problems, we would not grow."

−TONY ROBBINS

Your work is your passion and your heart; it taps into your deepest talents and purpose, and you feel blessed to be allowed to do this for a living! You hop out of bed (at least most mornings) to go to work and serve as you are called.

Then things seem to get more complex, and what you were doing yesterday isn't always working today. Your work begins to feel more like a burden than a joy. What might be happening is a growth step—how exciting! This means that it is time to pull back from the weeds, to step back and explore:

- What am I building?
- What actions do I need to take?
- What do I need to delegate?
- What are the high-level decisions that I need to make?

I have found that you really can't move forward with your important growth strategies *until* you recognize exactly where your business stands. These questions will help you get clearer about what is yours to do next. Once you have the answers (for yourself or with your people), you can begin to get strategic about your direction, delegating and hiring and adjusting programs and systems that will meet your new growth goals.

You can make empowered choices in business and life for your future when you know where you are and where you are called to go.

Inspiration by Rebecca Hall Gruyter, Influencer, Publisher and Animal Communicator

13.

Thought for the Day

"You must bloom wherever God plants you."

–TANIA SILVA

14.

Thought for the Day

"The way I see it, if you want the rainbow, you gotta put up with the rain."

–DOLLY PARTON

15.

Unlocking Your Prosperity

We might not remember when or where we first heard messages about money, but somewhere along the way, we internalized them and accepted them as truth. These "truths" then became part of our money stories and shaped the way we feel and think about money. The myths become part of our relationship with money.

One myth is that it's bad to focus on money, and only greedy people are concerned with money. This untruth makes us feel guilty or ashamed for wanting to be financially successful.

The truth is that you can have money—lots of it—and still be serving and living in alignment with who you are! Money can be used for good things or for not-good things. The paper dollars and metal coins that we call "money" are absolutely neutral. If you look for it, you can find proof that money is good, that it is okay to focus on money and that people who do are giving and doing amazing good in the world.

What you choose to do with money—how you define its importance in your own life—is where the power of money can be used to bring about good or evil. That choice is up to you!

What myths about money might you believe that are holding you back from reaching your full potential?

Inspiration by Rebecca Hall Gruyter, Influencer, Publisher and Animal Communicator

16.

Thought for the Day

"Life is like a coin. You can spend it any way you wish, but you only spend it once."

–LILLIAN DICKSON

17.

Feel the Fear and Crush It Anyway

Hey there, can we get real for a second? This whole "following your dreams" thing isn't all sunshine and daffodils. There are going to be days when the fear looms large, whispering those pesky what-ifs in your ear.

What if I fail spectacularly? What if I'm not cut out for this? What if the haters are right, and I'm just delusional? And maybe the biggest fear: What if I succeed?

I'll let you in on a little secret: Those fears will never go away completely. But you know what else won't go away? Your burning desire, your God-given talents and that undeniable spark that sets your soul on fire.

So feel the fear, lean into it and get cozy with those butterflies. They simply mean you care about what you're doing with all your heart; otherwise, would you get that ootz in your tummy? It's the price of admission to the wildest ride of your life.

Just look that fear straight in its quivering eyes and say, "Thanks for the adrenaline rush, but I've got dreams to chase!"

This month let's make fear our fuel. Every time self-doubt creeps in, use it as a reminder of what you're working toward-a life of passion, purpose and sweet, well-earned victory.

You've got this. Now go forth and conquer!

Inspiration by Janet Bernice Cheney, life-coach and best-selling author

18.

Show All Your Colors as You Bloom

There's joy in discovery, in showing up, in shining, in stretching to a new, exciting place.

In my own journey, I resisted being visible; I wanted to disappear. What have I discovered in being willing to be seen, going through being vulnerable, stripping away some of the layers I'd been hiding behind and really being seen exactly as I am?

It is actually freeing and joyful. I discovered that the "old way"—of acting a certain way, hiding parts of myself, following others' rules—takes a lot of energy. It drains our life away. And people can't really connect with us because we are not fully ourselves. **When we are willing to strip all that away and say, "*This is me!*" our energy increases, and people really lean in and connect. What joy that brings to everyone!**

Feeling joy and fun ties up all the other parts like a beautiful gift box. It keeps us remembering who we are, how colorful we are, what a wonderful light we shine. Laughter and joy are present-moment experiences that bring everyone together. How can you share more of yourself?

Inspiration by Rebecca Hall Gruyter, Influencer, Publisher and Animal Communicator

19.

Thought for the Day

"If you obey all the rules, you miss all the fun."
–KATHARINE HEPBURN

20.

Opportunity

"When one door of happiness closes, another opens, but often we look so long at the closed door that we do not see the one that has been opened for us."

−HELEN KELLER

Helen Keller's poignant words weave a tapestry of resilience and perspective. Having triumphed over monumental personal trials, Keller illuminates the truth that life's disappointments are mere passages, guiding us to new horizons. In moments of setback, we often find ourselves ensnared by what we have lost, rendering us blind to the possibilities that await. Her quote beckons us to redirect our gaze from past sorrows to future blessings, nurturing a spirit of hope and adaptability.

Within the realm of personal growth, this message radiates empowerment. It underscores the necessity of embracing a future-oriented mindset, welcoming new adventures even amidst adversity. By adopting this enlightened outlook, we can adeptly traverse life's inevitable ebbs and flows, understanding that each closed door is not an ending but a gentle nudge toward paths brimming with joy and fulfillment. Keller's wisdom softly whispers to keep our hearts and minds unlatched, ensuring we remain open to the exquisite opportunities that life perpetually unfolds before us. How can you stop looking at closed doors and be open to the new one that is opening?

Inspiration by Misti Mazurik, Author and Director of Operations at RHG Media Productions

21.

Celebration

My mom's birthday is in April. That is when we celebrate her birth as a human on Earth. I like this time of honor, celebration and reflection. I think we could all take time to celebrate having each other in our lives. How do you celebrate those beings in your life? Remember that there is great design and purpose and love that brings us to Earth, together and on our joined paths.

Inspiration by Pumpkin(g), the cat

22.

From Darkness to Light: Cultivating Hope and Resilience

Spring, with its gentle blossoms and vibrant hues, epitomizes hope's resurgence after the darkest of winters. Of the four seasons, Spring best symbolizes hope. It's a season of renewal, where life bursts forth from barren earth, reminding us that even in the coldest days, warmth and growth await.

To cultivate hope, let's shift our perspective like the changing seasons. Instead of dwelling on past failures or a dark past, let's embrace the lessons they offer and envision a future filled with beautiful experiences. Due to my abusive past, I spent most of my life focusing on the dark, operating from distorted perceptions of fear. I was not able to see the light or to feel hope.

I transformed my mindset from one of negativity to one of positivity and hope. I was able to see my experiences from the past as my badge of honor. I found resilience, wisdom and gratitude in the lessons learned. Hope enabled me to cross over the bridge of darkness to the light. Hope empowered me to activate the energy aligned with my desires, dreams and success.

Today I invite you to get out of your own way by shifting your mindset, focusing on gratitude, and stepping into the beautiful bright energy of hope!

Inspiration by Deborah Wiener, creator of The Energetic Business Feng Shui System™

23.

Thought for the Day

"No winter lasts forever; no spring skips its turn."

–HAL BORLAND

24.

Thought for the Day

"In life you get what you put in. When you make a positive impact in someone else's life, you also make a positive impact in your own life."

–MARCANDANGEL

25.

The Choices We Make

Even the choices we don't get to make can be stepping stones on the path that leads us to our purpose. Some of those choices that were made for us have been disempowering, abusive and even dangerous. So, how can they be stepping stones to good things? **I have discovered we can't always choose what happens to us, but we can choose our response.**

As a teenager, the seed of what my purpose would be was planted at a Women of Faith Conference, where I was inspired by the powerful women sharing their stories of hardship, tragedy and struggle, and how they chose to use their experiences to help and encourage other women. At that moment, I knew I wanted to be a motivational speaker, even though I was so fearful of being visible in any way, shape or form. I wanted my story and life to be used for good. The seed planted in my heart was that maybe, just maybe, my story could help another. That seed pulled me forward to overcome my fears, and today I have bloomed from the seeds of my purpose planted so long ago!

Perhaps you can relate to not feeling like you have a choice, that others are controlling your life and your destiny, that it's better to hide. **You still have a choice.**

Despite everything that may happen to you in your life, you do have at least one choice that is always yours to make. You can *still* be empowered and choose your response today and going forward! Your choices—your responses—can change the path of your life.

All of the things that happen to us can become the fuel that propels us toward our purpose.

Inspiration by Rebecca Hall Gruyter, Influencer, Publisher and Animal Communicator

26.

Thought for the Day

"Two roads diverged in a wood, and I – I took the one less traveled by, And that has made all the difference."

–ROBERT FROST

27.

Thought for the Day

"It only takes one person to make you happy and change your life: YOU."

–CHARLES ORLANDO

28.

The Gift of Forgiveness

"Forgive others, not because they deserve
forgiveness, but because you deserve bliss."

–MONEEKA SAWYER, THE BLISSFUL MILLIONAIRE

Forgiveness is a powerful tool that has the ability to bring peace and happiness into our lives. It is not always easy to forgive others, especially when we feel that they do not deserve it. However, holding onto anger and resentment only weighs us down and prevents us from experiencing true bliss.

When we choose to forgive others, we are not excusing their actions or denying the hurt they may have caused us. Instead, we are freeing ourselves from the burden of holding onto negative emotions. By letting go of anger and resentment, we create space in our hearts for love, compassion and joy to flourish.

Forgiveness is a gift we give ourselves. It allows us to move forward, heal and find inner peace. When we release those who have wronged us from the chains of our anger, we are ultimately setting ourselves free.

Remember to forgive others, not because they deserve it, but because you deserve to experience the beauty of bliss in your life. Today, whenever you start to feel that old familiar feeling of anger or a grudge, stop a moment and say to your anger, "I release you. In this moment I choose forgiveness, I choose peace and I choose happiness." Then take three deep breaths all the way down to your belly. Your heart will thank you for it.

Inspiration by Moneeka Sawyer, the Blissful Millionaire

29.

Thought for the Day

"Life is 10% what happens to me and 90% of how I react to it."

–CHARLES SWINDOLL

30.

Seeds of Bliss

"In the midst of adversity, plant the seeds of bliss;
from their roots will sprout the blossom of resilience,
ready to revolutionize your tomorrows."

−MONEEKA SAWYER, THE BLISSFUL REBEL

In challenging times, it's easy to feel overwhelmed and lose sight of the lighter side of life. But what if we viewed adversity as a moment to sow the seeds of joy? Let's remember that even in our darkest days, we have the power to cultivate positive outcomes.

Picture this: when faced with struggles, instead of sinking into despair, we can nurture small moments of happiness and gratitude. These might seem insignificant at first—like sharing a laugh with a friend, tending to a garden or finding solace in a good book. But these simple acts are the roots from which resilience can spring.

By intentionally choosing to embrace these tiny seeds of bliss, we set ourselves up for a transformation that reaches beyond today's worries. With time, patience, and a little bit of faith, those seeds will grow into a vibrant garden of bliss, strength and resilience, ready to bloom into a brighter tomorrow.

So, as we navigate life's ups and downs, remember: the power is within you to plant those seeds, nurture them and watch as they flourish. Embrace each moment, even the hard ones, because what you cultivate today will become the foundation of your strength for the future.

Inspiration by Moneeka Sawyer-The Blissful Rebel

May

1.

Create Bliss

"Bliss is not found, it's created. Choose to embrace the blissful moments in your life and they will continue to multiply."

–MONEEKA SAWYER, THE BLISSFUL MILLIONAIRE

In life, we often search for happiness and bliss as if they were hidden treasures waiting to be discovered. However, the truth is that bliss isn't something we stumble upon by chance-it's something we actively create and nurture within ourselves.

Every day, we have the power to choose what we focus on and how we react to the world around us. By consciously embracing the small moments of joy and gratitude that come our way, we are making a choice to invite more bliss into our lives.

Each smile, each laugh, each gesture of kindness has the potential to multiply and create a wave of positivity that touches not only our own hearts but those around us as well.

Today, as you navigate through your day, remember that bliss isn't a destination, it's a journey. Take a moment to pause, appreciate the beauty and joy that surrounds you, and watch as the blissful moments continue to grow and flourish in your day and life. Embrace the power you hold to create your own happiness.

Inspiration by Moneeka Sawyer, the Blissful Millionaire

2.

Thought for the Day

"Every adversity, every failure, and every heartache carries with it the seed of an equivalent or greater benefit."

–NAPOLEON HILL

3.

Success

"Success is getting what you want.
Happiness is wanting what you get."

–DALE CARNEGIE

Dale Carnegie, a luminary in the realm of self-improvement and the art of connection, encapsulates a timeless truth in his evocative quote. This profound statement elegantly delineates the distinction between the outward triumphs of success and the inner serenity of happiness. For Carnegie, success is often gauged by tangible milestones—reaching goals, amassing wealth or earning accolades. It embodies the pursuit of targets, demanding ambition, effort and unwavering determination.

Yet, happiness dances on a different wavelength. It transcends mere outcomes and blossoms as an intrinsic sense of fulfillment derived from cherishing what one already holds dear. This essence of happiness invites us to revel in the present, finding joy in life's simple pleasures, irrespective of external accomplishments. It thrives on gratitude and acceptance, offering a depth of satisfaction that success alone may not bestow.

Carnegie's wisdom illuminates the path of striving for success while nurturing a mindset that celebrates the present. This delicate equilibrium between aspiration and contentment is vital for holistic well-being. By embracing what you have, you shift your gaze from an endless pursuit to a profound appreciation of the now. Such a perspective fosters a harmonious existence where success and happiness entwine. Ultimately, Carnegie beckons us to realize that true contentment springs from aligning our external quests with our inner tranquility. What are you appreciating in the now?

Inspiration by Misti Mazurik, Author and Director of Operations at RHG Media Productions

4.

Thought for the Day

"The influence of a mother in the lives of her children is beyond calculation."

–JAMES E. FAUST

5.

Thought for the Day

"Not how long, but how well you have lived is the main thing."

–SENECA

6.

Thought for the Day

"A woman is like a tea bag – you never know how strong she is until she gets in hot water."

–ELEANOR ROOSEVELT

7.

Thought for the Day

"Step out of hiding onto the center stage of your life."

–REBECCA HALL GRUYTER

8.

Crystal Support

Did you know that crystals can support you? They come in different colors, vibrations and energy. They bring in wonderful healing qualities and energies that are beneficial.

You will actually be pulled to what you need . . . what calls to you or draws your attention? You already experience this all the time: your body tells you when you crave salt, the sunlight, chocolate. Similarly, your body will tell you what energy it needs, you just have to listen.

Try not to let your mind get involved when selecting something supportive but instead, go with your first instinct.

Inspiration by Jaimie Harnagel, Shaman

9.

Thought for the Day

*"You cannot afford to live in potential for the
rest of your life; at some point, you have to
unleash the potential and make your move."*

–ERIC THOMAS

10.

What the World Needs Is More of You

I believe every single person has been given unique talents, abilities, gifts and dreams. My vision is for everyone to have the chance to show up in just the way they are gifted to serve.

The world needs you in all your unique and wonderful ways!

I envision a big, beautiful gift box that I am handing to you right now. It is filled with reminders of who you are, how wonderful you are and the many ways that the world needs *you*. Take a moment to think about what it is inside the box—all the things that you love about yourself and others love about you, all the things that you were brought here to give to the world!

Take another moment to think about the joy and fun you have had—with your friends, with loved ones or all by yourself (which is a precious gift itself). Laughter and joy are present-moment experiences that bring our world together. The world can never have enough of our joy and laughter. The world can never have enough of *you*! **Remember to share the gift of you!**

Inspiration by Rebecca Hall Gruyter, Influencer, Publisher and Animal Communicator

11.

Cultivate Gratitude

"Let the revolution toward bliss begin not with the chase for happiness, but with the cultivation of gratitude in every moment."

–MONEEKA SAWYER, THE BLISSFUL REBEL

In our lives that often feel a relentless race for happiness, it's easy to lose sight of what truly matters. This quote reminds us that happiness isn't a destination, it's a byproduct of gratitude. Imagine starting each day by acknowledging the small things—your morning coffee, the warmth of the sun or the laughter of a loved one. These moments, when recognized, transform into threads of bliss woven into the fabric of our daily lives.

When we cultivate gratitude, we're not just ticking off a checklist, we're embodying a mindset shift. This revolution invites us to explore the beauty in imperfection. It encourages us to embrace the messy parts of life, teaching us that there's a lesson in every struggle and a silver lining in every challenge.

So, let your first action today be one of appreciation. Maybe jot down three things you're grateful for. As you nurture this practice, you'll find that the chase for happiness lessens, and instead, genuine bliss starts to flourish naturally. Let's embrace this revolution as a community, supporting each other to see the good in every moment. After all, when we shine our light of gratitude, it illuminates the path to bliss for ourselves and those around us.

Inspiration by Moneeka Sawyer-The Blissful Rebel

12.

Thought for the Day

"Your time is limited, so don't waste it living someone else's life. Don't be trapped by dogma – which is living with the results of other people's thinking."

–STEVE JOBS

13.

Your Message Is Needed!

When an opportunity comes to you to show up in a bigger way, it often means that you are being called to step out in ways you hadn't thought of before.

For many of the authors we help publish, it's their first time writing for the public. Typically, they have reached out to us from a deep soul place: "I'm being called to bring my mission forward. I want to reach the people I'm supposed to reach."

We work with them to bring that mission out into the world. What often happens when we start out is that the person doesn't even realize the power of what they are about to bring forward. They have fears about whether their message is worth hearing or their mission worth following. They don't realize how wonderful they are, but we do!

One of my greatest joys is when they launch their book out into the world, and it becomes a national or international best-seller. Not so much to accumulate awards, but because **they get to acknowledge and affirm the influence they are having in the world.** They get to see what others see, and when the world receives it so powerfully (whether it's a book, a presentation, a TV/radio show, etc.), this, in turn, is transformational for others. It's part of the journey that we take together of shifting and expanding how we show up in the world. How are you holding space for yourself and others to shine?

Inspiration by Rebecca Hall Gruyter, Influencer, Publisher and Animal Communicator

14.

Thought for the Day

"The most effective way to do it, is to do it."

–AMELIA EARHART

15.

Thought for the Day

"The best way to predict the future is to create it"

–ABRAHAM LINCOLN

16.

Thought for the Day

"Never be ashamed of what you feel. You have the right to feel any emotion that you want, and to do what makes you happy. That's my life motto."

–DEMI LOVATO

17.

Travel Communication

As you plan your trips, vacations and get togethers...remember those animals around you are listening. Hearing your plans, feeling your excitement or even travel nerves. They become concerned about having you out of their site and space. (For they chose you; you are their mission and they love you so.)

Let them know what is happening, that you are traveling. That you are going to rejuvenate, connect, celebrate, take break, visit so and so. Where you are going and most importantly that you will be back. Let them know when you'll be back...use the number of day's(sun's) and nights(moon's) (as they may not always understand dates and what a week means). Let them know who will care for them while you are gone and again most importantly when you will be home again. Be specific. It is up most important to them.

This communication will help ease their anxiety and reassure their hearts that they haven't lost you. You are precious to them dear one. This will also help you continue to grow closer and closer together. Enjoy your travels and remember to send them a virtual hug when they come to your heart and mind on your trip...they will also feel this love and connection too.

Inspiration by The Animal Council, from The Book Collective

18.

Thought for the Day

"It doesn't matter who you are, where you come from. The ability to triumph begins with you. Always."

–OPRAH WINFREY

19.

Thought for the Day

"Life is what happens when you're busy making other plans."

–JOHN LENNON

20.

Thought for the Day

"The only place success comes before work is in the dictionary."

–VINCE LOMBARDI

21.

Thought for the Day

"The only difference between an extraordinary life and an ordinary one is the extraordinary pleasures you find in ordinary things."

–VERONIQUE VIENNE

22.

Renewing Your Vibrancy: A May-jor Pep Talk

Question: Is your January goal still exciting? Yes or no, here's little pep talk to keep your vibrancy shining bright.

In January, we burst with fresh energy and New Year ambition. Our goals seemed so clear, our motivation unshakable. But now, a few months in, maybe that spark has fizzled a bit. The couch is oh-so-comfy, those old habits are whispering sweet nothings and your dreams feel . . .a little out of reach.

Here are some spiritual smelling salts . . . take a deep breath and remember why you started this journey in the first place. Was it to honor God with your gifts? To build a legacy for your loved ones? To finally, finally feel that sweet rush of "I did it!"?

Whatever your **why**, I'll bet it still sparks something deep within you. Lean into that feeling! Let it reignite your inner fire and send old doubts scurrying back into the shadows where they belong.

The path ahead won't be perfect-when is it ever?-but a few stumbles don't negate the progress you've already made. Shake off those missteps like the Sheroe (hero) you are, and stride forward. Acknowledge with joy how far you've come and have faith in how far you can go.

You've got this! Your vibrancy is eternal, an ever-renewing wellspring of passion and purpose. Now go forth and claim the life you were born for!

Inspiration by Janet Bernice Cheney, life-coach and best-selling author

23.

Thought for the Day

"Don't be afraid of the dark. Shine!"

–VERA NAZARIAN, THE PERPETUAL
CALENDAR OF INSPIRATION

24.

Polarities of Light and Dark

In the grand symphony of existence, the contrast between darkness and light orchestrates the melody of life, guiding us on a journey of profound self-discovery and growth. You can't have light without dark because the darkness leads us to the light. If you are willing and courageous enough to look at the dark, you will discover the wisdom that resides within you.

As you explore your dark shadow side, confront your fears, and clear the energy to emerge stronger and open the space to the light. It is within this spaciousness that we uncover the hidden gems of wisdom and insight, illuminating the path forward with newfound clarity and purpose. Within the depths of darkness lies the brilliance of our truest selves, awaiting discovery.

The light beckons us with its positive energy and radiance, reminding us of the boundless potential that resides within. It is in moments of connection, gratitude, and love that we experience the expansiveness of the universe, transcending the limitations of the human condition and embracing the vastness of our being.

As we navigate the ebb and flow of life, let us embrace the dance of darkness and light, knowing that each moment offers an opportunity for growth, transformation and self-realization. Embrace the spaciousness of existence, allowing it to guide you on a journey of profound discovery and the infinite possibilities that await you!

Life is a dance where darkness and light harmonize to reveal the beauty of balance and the richness of existence.

Inspiration by Deborah Wiener, creator of The Energetic Business Feng Shui System™

25.

Thought for the Day

"Don't ever underestimate the impact that you may have on someone else's life."

–ANONYMOUS

26.

Roots

Dear one, notice the trees...how we move and flow in the wind. We are able to stand firmly because our roots are deep and connected to the earth and to each other. We are able to bend, move and flow without breaking... again because our roots are firmly connected. You too can stand firm and bend in the wind and storm. To bend and flow but not break when your roots are deeply connected to the truth/source.

Grow your roots deeply and trust them to hold you firmly in any storm...and you too can learn to dance in the wind.

Inspiration by The Trees, from The Book Collective

27.

I AM...

I am safe.

I am enough.

<u>I am powerFULL.</u>

Inspiration by Jaimie Harnagel, Shaman

28.

Thought for the Day

"Your days are your life in miniature.
As you live your hours, so you create your years."

–ROBIN SHARMA

29.

Thought for the Day

*"In total darkness it only takes a
little light to shine the way."*

–ARI GUNZBURG, THE LITTLE BOOK OF GREATNESS:
A PARABLE ABOUT UNLOCKING YOUR DESTINY

30.

Patrol Your Boundaries

I am really good at protecting my home and those in it. I do this by guarding our perimeters to keep my family safe. I stay alert to what doesn't belong and notify my family. How are you protecting your boundaries? Pay attention to your boundaries; guard against negative or harmful energies and intentions that don't serve. Be diligent in protecting and honoring your boundaries. Remove negative or hurtful energies that don't belong. You are important and worth protecting.

Inspiration by Pumpkin(g), the cat

31.

Thought for the Day

"Life shrinks or expands in proportion to one's courage."

–ANAIS NIN

June

1.

Thought for the Day

"Genius is in the idea. Impact, however, comes from action."

–SIMON SINEK

2.

Animal Spirit Guides

Animal spirit guides are the animals in your life, or animals that cross your path. These animals have powerful and timely messages for you.

There is so much information on animal symbolism out there. You can do a search online and see what seeing different animals means. One great source is the book, *Animal Speak*, by Ted Andrews. It speaks to the messages different animals bring in so if an animal crosses your path or keeps appearing to you, whether in person or on TV or even in dreams, read up on what that animal symbolizes and see what message you find.

What are the special messages animals are giving you today?

What touches your heart and aligns with your spirit?

Inspiration by Jaimie Harnagel, Shaman

3.

Summer Is a Great Time to *Shine*!

We are halfway through the year, approaching Q3. I toast you with my fresh, minty, lemony iced tea. Here's to you!

And it's the perfect opportunity to take a look at where we are. Are we doing the things that matter most to us? Are we purposefully doing those things that bring us forward? Are we choosing to *shine* and echo out those things into our families, business, community and world?

Between the delicious summer moments of absorbing sunshine, eating barbeque, taking long walks, sitting with our summer reading books, also take some moments of reflection. Do a "check-in" on **what is important for you to build into your life that nourishes you, is positive and helps you grow.**

In what ways can you stay mindful of the types of things that get poured into you and to make sure they include practices that will uplift, feed, encourage and empower you?

This type of insight can come into your consciousness and become part of you, just like your wonderful memories of long summer evenings with loved ones and ice cream with friends on a hot day. Just remember to take time to stop, pause, listen and choose with purpose.

Inspiration by Rebecca Hall Gruyter, Influencer, Publisher and Animal Communicator

4.

The Power of Human Connection

The human need for connection goes beyond the physical; it is a universal energetic exchange essential to our survival as a species. The 2020 pandemic exasperated the epidemic of loneliness and separation, casting a shadow over our mental and emotional well-being. Yet, amidst the silence and solitude, there lies an opportunity for change by remembering that we are not here to be alone. "Connection is why we're here; it is what gives purpose and meaning to our lives," Brené Brown.

Overcoming separation begins with reaching out—to friends, family, community or organizations. The act of spending time together, being present, listening to each other and celebrating with others is invaluable. The moments you will remember at the end of your life will be the experiences and people you connected with.

Fitting in is not belonging, being accepted exactly as you are with unconditional love is belonging. Can you recall a time where you felt you truly belonged and the feeling of joy and aliveness it created within you? Being able to share moments of connection and belonging with others enriches our lives in profound ways.

Create a practice of reaching out and connecting, and together, we will overcome loneliness and create a world filled with love, connection and belonging! The greatest gift you can give someone is the gift of your time and attention.

Inspiration by Deborah Wiener, creator of The Energetic Business Feng Shui System™

5.

Choices

As a stick bug I am able to disguise myself, blend into my environment and get close to those things that matter to me. What I see when I look at humans are their amazing ability to choose their disguise, choose what they get close to and choose what they want to be part of. What are you choosing?

Inspiration by Twiggy, the Stick Bug, from The Book Collective

6.

Thought for the Day

*"be a wildflower
amongst cut flowers"*

–DAHI TAMARA KOCH

7.

Follow Your Heart

"In the land of conformity, be the vibrant color that sparks joy. A powerful rebel is not bound by rules, but uplifted by passion."

–MONEEKA SAWYER, THE BLISSFUL REBEL

In a world that often leans towards conformity, it's so easy to melt into the background like a gray shadow. But do you really want to live that way? The quote, "In the land of conformity, be the vibrant color that sparks joy," speaks directly to the heart of our individual journey. It whispers to us to embrace, accept and love our uniqueness—our quirks, talents and passions.

Think about it. Consider how breathtaking a sunset is with its layers of rich oranges, pinks and deep purples adorning the sky. That's how your vibrancy can impact those around you. When you dare to stand out, you not only inspire those around you but also create an environment filled with bliss and connection.

The second part of the quote reminds us that a powerful rebel isn't shackled by rules but instead energized by passion. It suggests that our passions serve as a driving force that can propel us forward, even when the path appears conventional or mundane.

So, let's color outside the lines and be the vibrant hues in an often monochrome world. Embrace your inner rebel, follow your heart and get ready to uplift not only yourself, but everyone around you. Today, how can you choose to spark joy in your world and the world of others?

Inspiration by Moneeka Sawyer-The Blissful Rebel

8.

Thought for the Day

"Stop wearing your wishbone where your backbone ought to be."

–ELIZABETH GILBERT

9.

Are You on a Mission to Shine?

My mission—the calling of my heart—is to help others know how valuable, gifted and wonderfully made they truly are. I think I knew this even as a little girl, and I followed different paths along the way to find where and how I was meant to shine. I even resisted it sometimes. When I heard God's soft voice in my ear, I would say, "No, not now, not yet!" Me, get up in front of people and speak when I can barely say my name out loud when someone asks? What, share my story in front of hundreds of people? Change my career and leap into something completely different, on my own?

Not now, not yet—or ever!

Yet, here I am today, shining my light and fulfilling my mission to serve in the best way that I'm able. Happier than I have ever been.

When we step forward and share the gift of us, we shine our light out into the world, rippling out rays of light wherever we go. Whether it's on our business, volunteer work, relationships with friends and family or a stranger on the street, you can be on a mission and share the gift of you with the world.

What is your mission? Where do you shine?

Inspiration by Rebecca Hall Gruyter, Influencer, Publisher and Animal Communicator

10.

Thought for the Day

"Recognize that every interaction you have is an opportunity to make a positive impact on others."

–SHEP HYKEN

11.

Thought for the Day

"Every strike brings me closer to the next home run."

–BABE RUTH

12.

Face the Sunshine

*"Keep your face always toward the sunshine
and the shadow will fall behind you."*

–WALT WHITMAN

Walt Whitman's quote serves as a profound metaphor for living an optimistic and forward-looking life. This evocative imagery suggests that by focusing on the positive aspects of life (the sunshine), the negative aspects (the shadows) will naturally recede into the background. Whitman, a celebrated American poet known for his humanist views, encapsulates a timeless piece of wisdom in this line.

The concept of facing the sunshine can be interpreted as maintaining a positive outlook, seeking opportunities and embracing hope. It encourages individuals to look ahead with confidence and not to dwell on past mistakes or the darker sides of life. This forward-facing perspective can be empowering, as it drives progress and personal growth. It suggests that by concentrating our energy on the good and the possible, we leave behind the negativity and challenges that might otherwise hold us back. The quote above underscores the importance of resilience and determination.

Ultimately, Whitman's words inspire a mindset that values perseverance and hope. They remind us that our focus and attitude can shape our experiences and outcomes. By choosing to face the sunshine, we align ourselves with a path of positivity and growth, ensuring that the inevitable shadows do not define our journey. Are you looking at the sunshine or the shadows?

Inspiration by Misti Mazurik, Author and Director of Operations at RHG Media Productions

13.

Thought for the Day

"Do what we can, summer will have its flies."
–RALPH WALDO EMERSON

14.

Thought for the Day

"I've always had a philosophy that position doesn't define power. Impact defines power. What impact are you making on people? What impact are you making on business?"

−MINDY GROSSMAN

15.

Play Matters

I LOVE to play and try to get those around me to play too! It's important! I even dream of adventures and ways to play. Play helps us to connect, raises our vibration, builds closeness and connection . . . and it is FUN! Humans sometimes don't play enough. They get too serious and heavy. Their energy and vibration dips.

The solution is to PLAY! Run, jump and find what is FUN for you. Create a game you love and enjoy! Laugh more, move, smile and love yourself in the game. Have fun and joy in life. Play more!

Inspiration by Pumpkin(g), the cat

16.

Thought for the Day

"One is loved because one is loved. No reason is needed for loving."

–PAULO COELHO, THE ALCHEMIST

17.

Courageous Bliss

"Don't live a life to avoid failure or getting hurt . .
.instead live life to experience unbridled bliss."

–MONEEKA SAWYER, THE BLISSFUL MILLIONAIRE

In life it's easy to stay safely tucked away from risks and challenges, but in doing so, we miss out on the opportunities for growth, the thrills of adventure and the joy of true fulfillment.

Instead of living in fear of hurt or failure, choose to be courageous, and open yourself up to a world of possibility, creativity and wonder. Yes, there may be moments of hurt or disappointment along the way, but those experiences will only make the moments of pure joy all the more sweet and precious.

Take a leap of faith into the unknown and let go of your fears. Embrace rejection and failure as steps towards your ultimate happiness. Your life should be filled with passion and purpose, so don't be afraid to chase after unbridled bliss in each moment. Remember, it's better to have loved and lost than to have never loved at all.

Today, go out there and whenever you have a moment of fear or hesitation, lean into it, and do that thing you're afraid of anyway. You'll be surprised what magic will unfold before your eyes.

Inspiration by Moneeka Sawyer, the Blissful Millionaire

18.

Thought for the Day

"I am in awe of flowers.
Not because of their colors,
but because even though they
have dirt in their roots,
they still grow.
They still bloom."

–D. ANTOINETTE FOY

19.

Redefining Success

As humans and as a society, we are taught that being busy and multitasking are an essential part of being successful. It is important to be "productive."

I would argue that perhaps what society considers a success i.e., being a doctor or a lawyer or a billionaire, is only that-an opinion of humans thinking on a material scale. While certain things are considered milestones on the ladder of success, I feel that these are very small in scale.

As we grow, we are taught, in large part, that being successful is more important than following your heart. We lose our dreams, we lose ourselves.

I feel that if you are a kind human being, if you lift others up, if you are helpful, if you make a difference in even ONE person's life, then you are successful.

This is, perhaps, the most impactful thing we can do, to make a difference for others.

Inspiration by Jaimie Harnagel, Shaman

20.

Shine Brightly in the World

What does shine brightly in the world mean to you?

For me, it starts with choosing what I believe in and for what I'm shining. With that clarity, I can then create the boundaries and support that will help me to stand firm and lift others up to move things in a positive direction.

I bring this clarity to my personal life and also to my business life. For me, the two are not separate from each other. For me, my business is part of my way of life.

What could shining brightly mean for your business (and life)? Could it mean:

- In every conversation, you allow the opportunity to lift up, support and really listen to others, whether it's a sales conversation or any other kind.

- You continue to move forward with confidence and power on opportunities in the ways you are being called to serve.

- You make a choice to be positive and forward-thinking, to be generous with your connections, introductions and how you serve. This is abundance thinking that is not competitive.

- You show up, share your time and skills, help society and the economy move forward (keep the energy of money circulating), even and especially in challenging times.

You feel good about yourself, satisfied with and gratified by how you have been a bright light today.

How are you choosing to shine each day, in each conversation and in each opportunity?

Inspiration by Rebecca Hall Gruyter, Influencer, Publisher and Animal Communicator

21.

Thought for the Day

"The best way to lengthen out our days is to walk steadily and with a purpose."

–CHARLES DICKENS

22.

Thought for the Day

"The question isn't who is going to let me; it's who is going to stop me."

−AYN RAND

23.

Thought for the Day

"Remember that the sun always shines even after stormy days."

–GIOVANNIE DE SADELEER

24.

Stop Being the Best-Kept Secret

This is your year. You are a beautiful, generous, gifted person who might be someone *that not many people know about* (meaning, a best-kept secret).

Are you top of mind for those people who need your positive impact? Can they easily find you, see you and hear you?

These are important questions to answer because I've discovered that if they cannot see you and hear you, then you cannot help them. This is why I believe **visibility is so very important** so that it's easy for people to find you.

This is also true: **There is no one out there who is magically going to put you on a stage, and then all your dreams are going to come true.** If you want to make a difference, you have to lead your own effort. If your visibility is low, then it's up to you to raise it—not anyone else but you.

The people who need your positive impact are waiting for you because *you are needed!* Believe me; people need you! People are hurting. People are discouraged. People are losing hope. People are praying and dreaming for somebody just like you to share with them your love, insight, wisdom and powerful gifts.

Can you make a commitment today to make yourself visible? To shine brightly enough so that your people can see your loving hand outstretched to help them?

Yes! No more hiding!

Inspiration by Rebecca Hall Gruyter, Influencer, Publisher and Animal Communicator

25.

Thought for the Day

"Every great dream begins with a dreamer. Always remember, you have within you the strength, the patience, and the passion to reach for the stars to change the world."

–HARRIET TUBMAN

26.

Thought for the Day

"You only live once, but if you do it right, once is enough."

–MAE WEST

27.

You *Are* the Star of Your Own Life

Hello shining stars! I hope you're ready for a little tough love this month as I impart some hard-won wisdom.

Too often, we get so caught up in pleasing others or meeting their expectations that we forget one crucial fact: This is **your** life, and you're the headliner! Not a supporting actor, not a background extra-the full-on star of the show.

Your dreams and desires are not deleted scenes from your life's movie lying on the cutting room floor. Why are we letting other people's opinions dictate the plot of our story?

This month, I challenge you to step into the spotlight and start playing the leading role you were born for. Kick those insecurities and self-doubts out of the director's chair and take the reins! Write your own script, filled with passion, purpose and as many sassy one-liners as you please.

And if anyone tries to heckle you from the cheap seats? Hit 'em with your signature hair toss and keep strutting because you own the stage—own that spotlight, shine!

You are a masterpiece crafted in the image of the Greatest Artist. So go ahead and take center stage-the world is waiting for the magic only you can give!

Inspiration by Janet Bernice Cheney, life-coach and best-selling author

28.

Thought for the Day

"It took me quite a long time to develop a voice and now that I have it, I am not going to be silent."

–MADELEINE ALBRIGHT

29.

Thought for the Day

"Be still and know that I am God."

−PSALM 46:10 (NIV)

30.

Thought for the Day

"Do not underestimate yourself by comparing yourself to others. It's our differences that make us unique and beautiful."

–RISHIKA JAIN

July

1.

Thought for the Day

"Shine your light and make a positive impact on the world; there is nothing so honorable as helping improve the lives of others."

–ROY T. BENNETT

2.

Happiness Is an Inside Job

"Happiness depends upon ourselves."

–ARISTOTLE

Aristotle's assertion that "Happiness depends upon ourselves" underscores the profound idea that our internal state largely dictates our sense of well-being. This perspective challenges the common belief that external circumstances, such as wealth, success or social approval are the primary sources of happiness. Instead, Aristotle suggests that happiness is a choice and a result of our attitudes, actions and decisions. By taking responsibility for our mental and emotional states, we empower ourselves to cultivate joy and contentment regardless of external conditions.

This philosophy encourages self-reflection and personal growth, urging us to develop virtues such as gratitude, resilience and kindness. It implies that by nurturing positive habits and mindsets, we can create a fulfilling life. For instance, practicing mindfulness and being present can help us appreciate the moment, while fostering meaningful relationships can provide a sense of connection and support. Additionally, setting and pursuing personal goals aligned with our values can bring a sense of purpose and satisfaction.

Aristotle's insight is timeless, reminding us that while we may not control all aspects of our lives, we do have the power to shape our reactions and attitudes. By focusing on what we can control and striving to improve ourselves, we lay the foundation for enduring happiness. In essence, true happiness is an inside job, and by nurturing our inner world, we can create a rich and rewarding life experience. What choices can you make today to nurture your inside world?

Inspiration by Misti Mazurik, Author and Director of Operations at RHG Media Productions

3.

Thought for the Day

"What you do has far greater impact than what you say."

–STEPHEN COVEY, AUTHOR AND EDUCATOR

4.

There's Plenty of Room for You to *Shine*!

There's room for everybody to shine. Life is not a competition.

There is enough space for everyone to bloom into the amazing individual that they uniquely are. Just look up into the night sky, the expansive universe. One star doesn't take away from the others; it just *is* and knows itself and shines like it's the only beautiful star out there. And it knows that it is part of something even more expansive and beautiful.

Just look at your garden. One bloom doesn't diminish the other—in fact, its brilliant red looks even more spectacular next to the bright yellow daisy next to it. Both shine even brighter!

People sometimes say to me, "But what do I have to say that hasn't already been said?" Or, "If I highlight this person, then everyone will go to them instead of me!"

I tell them, "There is nobody who says or does it exactly as you do. The world needs to hear you, and there is room for you and everyone else in a world of abundance."

The brighter you shine, the more that is seen, and the more good you can do in this world—as the unique gift that you are!

Inspiration by Rebecca Hall Gruyter, Influencer, Publisher and Animal Communicator

5.

Thought for the Day

"I've learned that people will forget what you said, people will forget what you did, but people will never forget how you made them feel."

–MAYA ANGELOU

6.

Choose Bliss

"You have the power to choose bliss in every moment. So why not make the choice that uplifts and energizes you."

–MONEEKA SAWYER, THE BLISSFUL MILLIONAIRE

In your life of endless choices, one of the most powerful decisions you can make is to choose bliss. Every moment presents you with an opportunity to pursue joy, to seek out the things that uplift and energize you.

Even when circumstances may seem difficult or out of our control, you still have the power to choose your mindset. It's easy to get caught up in the whirlwind of negativity and stress, but why not break free from that cycle and embrace the beauty of bliss instead?

By choosing to uplift and energize yourself, you are unlocking a world of endless possibilities and potential. You are setting the stage for a life filled with joy and fulfillment. So why not make the conscious decision to prioritize your own happiness?

Remember, you have the power within you to create the life you desire. So why not choose bliss in every moment, no matter how big or small? Embrace the choice that brings you closer to your true self and watch as your world transforms.

Today, what can you choose that will make you feel more blissful? Let bliss be your guiding light, leading you down a path of endless joy and fulfillment.

Inspiration by Moneeka Sawyer, the Blissful Millionaire

7.

Thought for the Day

"One of the most courageous things you can do is identify yourself, know who you are, what you believe in and where you want to go."

–SHEILA MURRAY BETHEL

8.

Thought for the Day

"To love beauty is to see light."

–VICTOR HUGO

9.

Nature

Now that I am an inside cat, I sometimes miss being outside. Connecting with nature, Gaia and other beings in the neighborhood. I miss having my paws on the earth. It grounds and centers me. As does connecting with the seasons . . . though I am not fond of being in the rain.

Sometimes my mom takes me outside and we enjoy sitting together in nature. This is good and important for all beings. Remember to take time to pause, put your paws on the ground. Connect, listen and breath in all that is around you.

Inspiration by Pumpkin(g), the cat

10.

Thought for the Day

"Do not go where the path may lead, go instead where there is no path and leave a trail."

–RALPH WALDO EMERSON

11.

Your Vibrant Self

Can you feel that summer energy thrumming through your veins? July has arrived, and it's bringing a fresh wave of vibrancy to renew our spirits.

I don't know about you, but there's something about this month that awakens my inner firecracker. Maybe it's the sunshine igniting my soul or the hot temps turning up the heat on my motivation. Whatever the reason, I'm ready to live the most vibrant life yet!

This July let's promise ourselves that we are going to continue to chase our dreams and do it with wild abandon. Kick self-doubt's and sashay forward in total, "You can't dim this shine" confidence.

Because here's the truth: You, my friends, are unstoppable forces of nature. Radiant souls crafted in the image of the Greatest Artist, overflowing with gifts the world can't wait to receive. So let's spend this month pouring out those gifts without apology or restraint.

Whether your vibrancy takes the form of creative expression, entrepreneurial hustle or simply being the light in someone's day, let it shine, let it shine, let it shine! The path won't be perfect, but every stumble is just a chance to pick yourself up and shimmy onward.

Because, really, what if everything we are going through is just preparing us for what we dream of doing, creating, being?

You've got this. Now go forth and set the world ablaze with your brilliance!

Inspiration by Janet Bernice Cheney, life-coach and best-selling author

12.

Thought for the Day

"A friend is a gift you give yourself."
–ROBERT LOUIS STEVENSON

13.

Choose Your Frequency

Pay attention to your energy; your vibration. What are you operating at? A lower negative energy or one that is positive, powerful and loving? You can choose your frequency; the level you vibrate at and share with the world.

Inspiration by The Crystalline Council, from The Book Collective

14.

Thought for the Day

"The only person you are destined to become is the person you decide to be."

–RALPH WALDO EMERSON

15.

Learn to Dance with Fear

Have you ever noticed that the more you try to avoid fear, the more it seems to grow and take you over? I have learned to "dance" with fear— move with it and through it, not avoid or run from it.

Think of fear as an indicator of stepping out of your familiar comfort zone into a new place. If you want to go where you haven't been before and serve in new ways, then you're choosing to move out of your comfort zone.

It is your choice to move forward or stay where you are.

Be willing to be a little uncomfortable (for a while) to build what you're called to build and be what you're called to be. What helps me through my fear is remembering my "why" and that my choice is voluntary. I just take one step at a time, pulled forward by my purpose of bringing truth, empowerment, choice and value into someone's life.

Fear is temporary; the rewards of the dance last a lifetime!

Inspiration by Rebecca Hall Gruyter, Influencer and Empowerment Leader

16.

Thought for the Day

*"If life were predictable it would cease
to be life, and be without flavor."*

–ELEANOR ROOSEVELT

17.

A Ripple in Water

Be kind to everyone.

I know this can be challenging if you come across someone who is mean or rude, but we don't know what their challenge is or what they are going through in that moment.

IF we can shift that energy for them by a kind word or smile (yes, even if it is not reciprocated!), their day will go a little differently and in turn, everyone they come into contact with. All of a sudden you have a beautiful domino effect, and whether you are aware of it or not, it can make a huge impact. A pebble making a ripple in the water.

Sometimes having compassion and holding space for others is the most impactful thing you can do.

And not to dismiss any personal gain . . . I know I have walked away from many a small exchange with a huge smile on my face. These interactions also raise my vibration!

Inspiration by Jaimie Harnagel, Shaman

18.

It's Not Your Job to Please Everybody, Is It?

I discovered that it's not my job to please everybody—it sounds simple, doesn't it? As vulnerable as that might make you feel, know that you cannot step onto center stage as an expert or influencer without taking a stand, and that stand simply won't please everybody!

You know and keep your boundaries and go forward with the awareness that people will say and feel a lot of things about you and your business. **Don't get caught up in what others say. Stay aware and observe where there's truth and where there isn't.**

Take in what will serve your brand, business and life, and kindly release what will not. One phrase I've found that helps me keep my boundaries is: "I can really see how you feel this way; however, this is what we do here."

Be willing to lead and bring forward all you are called to bring forward. Stand in your truth and shine!

Inspiration by Rebecca Hall Gruyter, Influencer, Publisher and Animal Communicator

19.

Thought for the Day

"Do not dwell in the past, do not dream of the future,
concentrate the mind on the present moment."

–BUDDHA

20.

The Freedom to Choose Bliss

"The power of choice is the ultimate freedom. Choose to create a life filled with love, laughter and bliss."

–MONEEKA SAWYER, THE BLISSFUL MILLIONAIRE

In life, we are faced with countless decisions and choices every single day. These choices have the power to shape our future and determine the path we take. It is in these moments of decision-making that we truly discover the power of choice, the ultimate freedom that lies within our grasp.

Each day, we have the opportunity to choose to create a life filled with love, laughter and bliss. We have the power to choose to surround ourselves with positive energy, to let go of negativity and to embrace each moment with open arms and a grateful heart.

When we choose to live a life filled with love, we invite bliss into our lives. When we choose to embrace laughter and find humor in even the most difficult situations, we lighten our hearts and lift our spirits. And when we choose to seek out moments of bliss and contentment, we discover the beauty in the world around us.

Today, I urge you to exercise the power of choice in your life. Choose to cultivate thoughts filled with love, laughter and bliss. Choose to see each situation today from the filters of abundance, happiness and fulfillment. The power is within you, so embrace it and live the life of bliss you truly deserve.

Inspiration by Moneeka Sawyer, the Blissful Millionaire

21.

Thought for the Day

"Continuous effort -- not strength nor intelligence -- is the key to unlocking our potential."

–WINSTON CHURCHILL

22.

Morning Mindset

*"Start your day with a devotion to the Bliss Revolution—
bend the arc of your thoughts toward bliss, and
watch how the world begins to bend in return."*

–MONEEKA SAWYER, THE BLISSFUL REBEL

Have you ever noticed how your morning mindset can shape the rest of your day? Today I invite you to consciously cultivate joy within yourself before stepping out into the world.

Imagine waking up each morning and taking a moment to embrace your thoughts, focusing on the little things that bring you joy. Maybe it's the warmth of your coffee, the soft light filtering through your window or the comforting knowledge that a new day is filled with possibilities. By dedicating ourselves to finding bliss in these details, we support our journey toward inner peace and happiness.

As we shift our focus to joy, we create a ripple effect—one that inspires our interactions and experiences throughout the day. Suddenly, the mundane can become magical, and challenges transform into opportunities for growth.

So, why not embrace this Bliss Revolution? This morning begin with a mindset that seeks joy, celebrates life and acknowledges the beauty around us. And if you can do this each morning, soon enough, you might find the world reflecting that very bliss back to you.

Inspiration by Moneeka Sawyer-The Blissful Rebel

23.

Thought for the Day

"We are all faced with a series of great opportunities brilliantly disguised as impossible situations."

–CHUCK SWINDOLL, CHRISTIAN
PASTOR AND RADIO PREACHER

24.

Thought for the Day

"You don't get to choose how you're going to die. Or when. You can only decide how you're going to live. Now."

–JOAN BAEZ

25.

Thought for the Day

"Patience is the calm acceptance that things can happen in a different order than the one you have in mind."

–DAVID G. ALLEN

26.

Thought for the Day

"The whole secret of a successful life is to find out what is one's destiny to do, and then do it."

–HENRY FORD

27.

Harmony in Connection: Nurturing Beautiful Bonds

In the garden of life, relationships are the most delicate and cherished blooms. Just as flowers require tender care, so do our connections with others. To foster beautiful, healthy relationships, remember this: communication is the water that nourishes the roots, trust is the soil that anchors growth and empathy is the sunlight that helps love blossom.

Cultivating harmony in our relationships enriches our souls, brings warmth, joy and fulfillment, requiring awareness of our thoughts, words and actions. The practice of active listening requires truly hearing what your partner, friend or loved one is saying without judgment or interruption, fostering understanding and deepening the connection between hearts.

As the Dalai Lama wisely said, "Love and compassion are necessities, not luxuries. Without them, humanity cannot survive." Let your thoughts, words and actions be guided by kindness, compassion and love. Let your presence be a sanctuary, a safe space where others can flourish and be themselves.

Moving with grace, honoring each other's uniqueness and embracing the beauty of togetherness brings love and understanding, weaving the most magnificent energetic patterns. Conscious evolution will attract the magnetic forces of positive energy to blossom into beautiful bonds that emanate harmony, love and joy.

Inspiration by Deborah Wiener, creator of The Energetic Business Feng Shui System™

28.

Thought for the Day

"Life is not measured by the number of breaths we take, but by the moments that take our breath away."

−MAYA ANGELOU

29.

Polish Your Light to Shine Even Brighter

Periodically, it's important to take some time to step back from the weeds and think about *you*.

Look at what excites you about your business. It may involve reminding yourself of your original mission and purpose in getting into this business. You may discover something that you thought was important at the beginning but is not so important or within your focus now. Notice whether or not you would miss that thing if you released it.

Think about what keeps rising to the top for you—is it something that your customers are asking for consistently? Is it something you're feeling called to do, like speak on stage or write a book? Is it a new direction you can begin to set a vision to achieve down the road in a few months or years? Is it a shift in your role as ambassador of your brand (the "face" of the company)? Are you feeling that your brand could benefit from your taking less of a customer-facing role or a more visible role?

These are all considerations that are important to contemplate, journal about and maybe discuss with people close to you whom you trust. It's worth the time so that you can be sure you are moving in the right direction with your growth plan.

Inspiration by Rebecca Hall Gruyter, Influencer, Publisher and Animal Communicator

30.

Thought for the Day

"Whatever your passion is, keep doing it. Don't waste chasing after success or comparing yourself to others. Every flower blooms at a different pace."

–SUZY KASSEM

31.

Thought for the Day

"You miss 100% of the shots you don't take."

–WAYNE GRETZKY

August

1.

Thought for the Day

"No matter what you look like or think you look like you're special and loved and perfect just the way you are."

–ARIEL WINTER

2.

Boundaries as Sanctuaries: Honoring Self and Others

A pivotal moment occurred when I was helping my son move into his first college dorm room and he felt overwhelmed by my excessive "help." It prompted a vital reassessment of my relationship and understanding of boundaries. Discovering boundaries as sacred lines that honor self and others pave the way to more harmonious relationships. This awareness brought me to the realization I was overstepping my son's boundaries and not showing him respect or trust.

You may perceive boundaries as mere physical barriers, but they really are powerful energies not walls; sanctuaries fostering mutual respect and understanding. Setting boundaries isn't always a walk in the park. Often, it's our own inner demons—fear of abandonment, rejection, or loss—that hold us back. But remember, every step toward setting boundaries is a step toward reclaiming your power and honoring your worth.

The practice of setting boundaries requires clarity, assertiveness, and compassion. Clarity involves articulating needs and limits, while assertiveness means confidently communicating boundaries with respect. Setting boundaries creates a ripple effect of positive energy in your relationships and endeavors.

As Oprah Winfrey once said, "You teach people how to treat you by what you allow, what you stop and what you reinforce." Embrace the power of boundary-setting as a transformative practice that elevates your energy, empowers your sense of self-worth and fosters self-respect. With each boundary you set, may you step into your personal power and cultivate a life filled with harmony, authenticity and empowerment.

Inspiration by Deborah Wiener, creator of The Energetic Business Feng Shui System™

3.

Thought for the Day

"I will never have this version of me again.
Let me slow down and be with her."

–ALWAYS EVOLVING

4.

Impossible

"Nothing is impossible. The word itself says 'I'm possible!'"

–AUDREY HEPBURN

Audrey Hepburn's quote is a powerful reminder of the limitless potential within each of us. This statement is the essence of optimism and the boundless human spirit. Hepburn, a celebrated actress and humanitarian, encourages us to reframe our perspective on challenges and obstacles. By breaking down the word "impossible" into "I'm possible," she illustrates that our mindset plays a crucial role in overcoming difficulties. This clever play on words invites us to see possibilities where we might otherwise perceive barriers.

The quote is a testament to the power of positive thinking. It suggests that our beliefs about our capabilities can profoundly impact our actions and outcomes. When faced with daunting tasks, it's easy to feel overwhelmed and defeated. However, Hepburn's insight prompts us to shift our focus from limitations to opportunities. By embracing this perspective, we can unlock new pathways to success and innovation.

Moreover, this quote resonates beyond personal growth; it applies to broader societal challenges as well. In a world where we often confront seemingly insurmountable issues, from climate change to social justice, Hepburn's words remind us that collective effort and a can-do attitude can lead to meaningful progress. Her message is one of empowerment and hope, encouraging us to believe in ourselves and our ability to affect change. What change are you leaning into? As you are possible!

Inspiration by Misti Mazurik, Author and Director of Operations at RHG Media Productions

5.

Thought for the Day

"Winter is an etching, spring a watercolor, summer an oil painting and autumn a mosaic of them all."

–STANLEY HOROWITZ

6.

Thought for the Day

"August is the time when you can have your cake and eat it too – with ice cream on the side."

–LIZA VORSTER

7.

Blissfully Overcoming Challenges

"True bliss is not the absence of struggles, but the unwavering belief that joy and contentment are always inside you to tap into."

–MONEEKA SAWYER, THE BLISSFUL MILLIONAIRE

With challenges and obstacles, it's easy to fall into the mindset that happiness is something we must constantly strive for outside of ourselves. But in truth, bliss lies not in the absence of struggles, but in the unwavering belief that joy and contentment are always within your reach.

Happiness isn't about avoiding hardships or difficulties but about harnessing the power that lies within you to find peace and fulfillment despite them. It's about recognizing that true bliss lies not in external circumstances but in your own mindset and attitude towards life.

When you approach each day with positivity and gratitude, you open yourself up to the endless possibilities of bliss. So, when challenges come your way, remember that true bliss is not something you need to chase after, it's something you already possess, deep within your core.

Today, whenever you face a challenge, take three deep breaths and ask yourself, "Is there anything about this I can be grateful for?" If yes, then focus on that gratitude for a few moments before you move forward to handle the challenge. If no, then ask, "What can I be grateful for in this moment?" And focus for a few moments on something you feel truly grateful for. Then tackle your task. See how much lighter your challenge feels in your mind and body.

Inspiration by Moneeka Sawyer, the Blissful Millionaire

8.

Thought for the Day

"You have brains in your head. You have feet in your shoes. You can steer yourself any direction you choose... And YOU are the one who'll decide where to go."

–DR. SEUSS, "OH, THE PLACES YOU'LL GO!"

9.

Thought for the Day

*"When you get the choice, to sit it out
or dance, I hope you dance."*

–LEE ANN WOMACK, "I HOPE YOU DANCE"

10.

Thought for the Day

"Remember who you are. Don't compromise for anyone, for any reason. You are a child of the Almighty God. Live that truth."

–LYSA TERKEURST

11.

Music Feeds the Soul

Ah, August. The end of summer nears . . . what awaits you in the fall and winter?

We all know that feeling where a song from our youth comes on, and all of sudden, we are right back there in high school or college.

Hearing one note can take you back to your past or impact your present by shifting your emotional state in an instant.

I find it freeing to blast tunes in the car and sing along. (You Gen Xers out there know exactly what I'm talking about!)

Music feeds the soul and it has the ability to make you feel alive and transport you.

Create space for it and you will find your joy.

Inspiration by Jaimie Harnagel, Shaman

12.

Thought for the Day

"The unexamined life is not worth living."

–SOCRATES

13.

Come Out of Hiding and *Shine*!

This means that **we can't hide behind the roles that we play, our credentials or our limiting beliefs.** These things, which we believe are protecting us, actually block people from truly hearing and experiencing us—the very people who need us are separated from us.

The only way to be found is for you to **be willing to take off all that stuff that is blocking the connection.** The only way to truly make a positive difference in the world is to **be willing to be seen authentically and transparently.**

I invite you today to look at ways in which you might be hiding a little bit. Please do this without self-judgment or criticism and always with self-love.

And then ask: In what ways could I step out of hiding onto the center stage of my life just a little bit more?

A great first step is to decide on an action you could take today to lean into making a difference for another and to shine your light for them.

Inspiration by Rebecca Hall Gruyter, Influencer, Publisher and Animal Communicator

14.

Thought for the Day

"A leader is a dealer in hope."
–NAPOLEON BONAPARTE, FRENCH
MILITARY LEADER AND EMPEROR

15.

Passion

Do you wake up and can't wait to start the day because of what awaits you? If not, why? What can you do about it? And why would you wait to start?

"Follow your passion. That's the compass needle that allows you to follow your true north.

That's the link that allows you to align with your true self. Follow the love, follow the passion . . . that's who you are." -Bashar

When you combine your passion and your truth, you fall into perfect alignment.

So, what are you passionate about?

How can you live that passion today in your words, actions and way of being?

Inspiration by Jaimie Harnagel, Shaman

16.

Thought for the Day

"Be faithful in small things because it is in them that your strength lies."

–MOTHER TERESA

17.

Thought for the Day

"Problems are not stop signs, they are guidelines."

–ROBERT SCHULLER

18.

How Your Ancestors Teach You to *Shine*

I am fortunate to have had wonderful relationships with four grand-mothers who richly blessed me and impacted my life. They each, in their own way, inspired the shape and form of the work I get to do in the world.

When, as a child, I didn't feel very good about myself, one grandmother taught me to give myself the same grace, love and understanding as I would for my very best friend. Another taught me not to wait for permission but to step into who I am authentically and powerfully. From another, I learned to work hard for what truly matters to me and always to walk with honor and integrity. And another taught me the importance of lifting others up and how we can all make a positive difference, heart by heart and life by life.

I'm thankful for their legacy and the gift of having them in my life. I think with wonder about what each of my grandmothers learned from *their* elders in ways that influenced the persons they would become—and on and on, back through time, each generation standing on the shoulders of the one before them!

Who in your life has influenced and inspired you along your journey? Take a moment now to think about them, celebrate them and send your love and gratitude their way. **We don't walk alone on this journey, and the more we open ourselves up to remembering those who walked beside us, the more we bring out their powerful gifts to guide us.**

Inspiration by Rebecca Hall Gruyter, Influencer, Publisher and Animal Communicator

19.

Thought for the Day

"Even the darkest night will end and the sun will rise."

–VICTOR HUGO

20.

Thought for the Day

"Everything has its wonders, even darkness and silence, and I learn, whatever state I'm in, therein to be content."

–HELEN KELLER

21.

Joyful Heart

"The Bliss Revolution is not just a movement; it's a commitment to finding beauty in the mundane and uplifting others with the limitless power of joy."

–MONEEKA SAWYER, THE BLISSFUL REBEL

Have you ever considered how much beauty surrounds us in our everyday lives? In our fast-paced lives, it's easy to overlook the small moments that bring us happiness. But what if we shifted our perspective and made it our mission to find joy in the everyday rhythm of life? Whether it's savoring your morning tea, stealing a smile from a stranger, or simply taking a moment to appreciate the colors of nature, there's beauty waiting to be discovered.

The Bliss Revolution encourages us to lift one another up, recognizing the transformative power of kindness and love. When we commit to sharing our joy, we create ripples that extend beyond ourselves, inspiring others to do the same. Imagine how wonderful our communities would be if we celebrated our victories, big and small, together!

I invite you to be part of this revolution—one small act of joy at a time. After all, a joyful heart is contagious, and in our commitment to find bliss in the ordinary, we can change lives, including our own.

Inspiration by Moneeka Sawyer-The Blissful Rebel

22.

Thought for the Day

"Do your little bit of good where you are; it's those little bits of good put together that overwhelm the world."

–DESMOND TUTU

23.

Be, Hug and Love

It is important to be present and in the moment. Hug deeply and fully and love with your full heart. We would all feel more love and connection if we would hug a little longer, show our love a little more and choose to be truly present in the moment with each other.

I feel most loved when I am held, hugged and feel the focus of love on me. (I call it a "Love Beam" . . . love beaming right to me and my heart.) In that moment, I know all is well and that I am truly loved. And so are you.

Share and receive love beams. They are truly powerful and can give your heart safety, courage, hope and love. Your heart will thank you! You will feel truly seen, heard and loved.

Inspiration by Pumpkin(g), the cat

24.

Thought for the Day

"Let us remember: One book, one pen, one child, and one teacher can change the world."

–MALALA YOUSAFZAI

25.

Thought for the Day

"You can never have an impact on society if you have not changed yourself."

−NELSON MANDELA

26.

Thought for the Day

"It's never too late to be what you might have been."

–GEORGE ELIOT, PEN NAME FOR MARY ANN EVANS

27.

Step Forward in Your Relationship with Money

Sometimes we have this "thing" about money. Many people know we have to deal with it, but we'd really rather not have to talk about it; we just hope that everything falls into place.

So we get disconnected from money. We leave money out of the conversation about our intentions, our goals and our wants, which makes it hard for money to support our intentions, goals and purpose.

I want to encourage you to instead purposely build a relationship, an ongoing conversation, with money. Let money in on what you want from it! Open your ears; listen to what's being offered to you. You can see what serves you and what does not: What do you really need? What do you want to build and create? What matters to you? Let money be part of what you are looking to build and create: a valued and trusted partner.

Discover how to connect with money, communicate with money, and build what matters most to you with money coming alongside to support you. Remember, money doesn't get to direct the relationship—you get to choose. Choose to build a positive relationship with money.

Inspiration by Rebecca Hall Gruyter, Influencer, Publisher and Animal Communicator

28.

Come Outside

Dear one, remember to come outside. To walk, laugh, and play. Connect with me, with the earth. Listen to my wisdom and feel my support and love. Fee the air. Walk upon the dirt and see what is all around you...that you are part of and is part of you.

Breathe in the fresh air and feel it support you. Cleaning out the old and making room and space for the new. See the beauty around you. Open you heart and spirit to hear the messages I have for you. See the beauty all around you and let it nurture your heart and spirit.

I whisper messages to your heart. Messages of love, support, insight, clarity and purpose. Come outside and walk with me. Sit with me. Grow with me.

Inspiration by Gaia, Mother Earth, from The Book Collective

29.

Thought for the Day

"The only limit to your impact is your imagination and commitment."

–TONY ROBBINS

30.

Thought for the Day

"In the middle of difficulty lies opportunity."

–ALBERT EINSTEIN

31.

A Harvest of New Beginnings: Embrace It

There's a subtle energy shift in the air, can you feel it? August has arrived, and with it comes the first whispers of transition-a reminder that all things must change.

For some, this might feel like a melancholy time, the slow fade of summer's warmth into autumn's crisper breezes. But in that bittersweet surrender, there's also profound beauty waiting to be uncovered.

Because just like the trees shedding last year's leaves to prepare for fresh growth, August ushers in a season of rebirth. A chance to let go of what no longer serves us and make space for new dreams to take root

So let's embrace this sacred pause between seasons, shall we? Use it as a time to go inward, to reflect on where you've been and where you hope to journey next. Maybe there are old habits or mindsets that need releasing, like those autumn leaves returning to the earth. Maybe there are fresh goals or passions whispering to be nurtured into bloom.

Whatever this transition sparks within you, treat it as a holy invitation-one from the Greatest Artist, beckoning you to cocreate something wildly beautiful. Have the courage to prune away the deadwood and clear space for your most vibrant self to emerge, radiant and renewed.

The seasons are changing, my friends, but your brilliance is eternal. So, take a deep breath, feel that delicious crispness in the air and step bravely into your next glorious becoming.

Inspiration by Janet Bernice Cheney, life-coach and best-selling author

September

1.

You Were Made for Such a Time as This, Therefore, *Shine*!

"If not now, when?"

–HILLEL, THE ELDER

Things happen in our lives that we don't expect and certainly didn't choose—a car accident, a divorce, a job loss or illness. "Such a time as this" could be an opportunity. We may not have chosen the event, but **we can choose how we are going to respond: to suffer or shine!**

These times may have us answering questions we don't often answer until we're faced with the possible end of ourselves. These are times when we get to ask **what matters most to us and how do we make that move forward and serve us?**

Life events challenge us to respond from an empowered place, to rethink things and to realize that time is precious.

Wherever you are in your journey, wherever you're being called, remember, it's now, it's today. Tomorrow isn't guaranteed. We have now.

What action can you take today to help you move forward that matters most to you?

Inspiration by Rebecca Hall Gruyter, Influencer, Publisher and Animal Communicator

2.

Thought for the Day

"The two most important days in your life are the day you are born and the day you find out why."

–MARK TWAIN

3.

Thought for the Day

"Our daily decisions and habits have a huge impact upon both our levels of happiness and success."

–SHAWN ACHOR

4.

Bliss

"Bliss is not about getting everything you want, but about appreciating everything you have."

–MONEEKA SAWYER, THE BLISSFUL MILLIONAIRE

In our society that equates success and happiness with material wealth, it can be easy to lose sight of what truly matters. The pursuit of more, bigger, better can lead to a never-ending cycle of desire and being perpetually unsatisfied. Bliss, however, is not found in the accumulation of more possessions but in the simple moments of appreciation for what we already have.

True bliss is a state of being that is not dependent on external circumstances or material wealth. It is a mindset that is cultivated through the practice of gratitude for the simple moments that make life meaningful. Practicing gratitude is about shifting our focus from what we lack to what we have. When we pause to reflect on the blessings in our lives, no matter how small they may seem, we open ourselves up to a sense of fulfillment. The warmth of a loved one's smile, the beauty of a flowering tree or the comfort of a warm cup of tea on a cold day-these are the moments that create a deep sense of peace and fulfillment that transcend material wealth and give us lasting joy.

Today, take a moment to pause, breathe and savor the beauty of the world around you. In this state, write down at least three things you notice. True bliss is waiting to be discovered in the moments of gratitude that fill your life.

Inspiration by Moneeka Sawyer, the Blissful Millionaire

5.

Thought for the Day

"A relationship that is truly genuine does not keep changing its colors. Real gold never rusts. If a relationship is really solid and golden, it will be unbreakable. Not even Time can destroy its shine."

–SUZY KASSEM

6.

Crystals

I LOVE crystals! They are always supportive of me and their connection helps me center and clear negative energies (or meanies as I call them). They help support all that we are and do. One of my favorite crystals is rose quartz. It soothes, heals, shares the vibration of love and always makes me feel better. And I love selenite too! It always clears away negative/heavy energy and gives me positive energy, making me feel good.

What crystals can you bring into your life? What support are you looking for?

Inspiration by Pumpkin(g), the cat

7.

Thought for the Day

"To love oneself is the beginning of a lifelong romance."

–OSCAR WILDE

8.

Your Spirit Tribe

Ask for help.

You are born with a Guardian Angel and your Power Animal is with you throughout your life.

Reach out to your power animals, your spirit guides, the angelic realm, to Spirit. Ask for help.

Remember, you are never alone.

Angels are always with us but cannot interfere unless you ask for help.

And remember, you can reach out to God at any time. You don't necessarily have to be a religious person to be spiritual. God is everywhere, in everything. Always accessible.

Call in your Spirit Tribe!

How can you ask for help today?

Inspiration by Jaimie Harnagel, Shaman

9.

Thought for the Day

"Greater love has no one than this, that someone lay down his life for his friends."

–JOHN 15:13 (NASB)

10.

Stop. Breathe. Check-in.

Do you ever have periods in your work or business where it feels like a blur, when things just keep moving at a speeding pace, and you never quite get control of things or have a handle on what just happened?

In these times, our heads are full, stress-producing hormones are rising, time seems to fly and we forget ourselves. We forget to breathe, to be present, to be mindful of the wonderful gift that we are. Here are some ways that I have learned and shared with others to be more present in every precious moment of life.

Stop and remember why you are here. You are here on purpose, and you have a purpose for everything you do—right at this moment and this one and this one.

Remind yourself of who you are and how wonderful you are. How beautiful and unique you are and how you show up in the world.

Be present to your experience. Before you start an activity or attend an event or even just starting your day, take some moments to ask yourself: "What is it that I need to know or to have today? What is it that will encourage me, equip me, empower me to bring in my magic [in this activity]?"

There's real power in stopping and checking in with yourself. It helps keep you grounded and clear, no matter what. Remember to stop, pause and breathe.

Inspiration by Rebecca Hall Gruyter, Influencer, Publisher and Animal Communicator

11.

Thought for the Day

"Darkness enables us to shine."

–STEVEN MAGEE

12.

Thought for the Day

"You don't have to remind a flower when its time to bloom is near; it has been preparing for it all of its life."

–MATSHONA DHLIWAYO

13.

Raise Your Vibration

Everything has energy. Energy vibrates and cycles, which creates frequency. Raising our consciousness and our vibration means we feel lighter.

When our vibration is high, we think clearer, and we are able to stand in our own personal power. Things flow easier, everything falls into alignment.

Here are some ways to shift your vibration:

Listen to music or play drums or any instrument for that matter (sound healing). Have colorful or inspirational art that speaks to you around your space, (visual healing), apply color therapy, partner with crystals, movement . . . get up and dance! Or do yoga. Get outside in nature, even for a few minutes. If done with intention, all these (and more) will bring about a shift in your energy quickly.

Inspiration by Jaimie Harnagel, Shaman

14.

Mistakes

"A person who never made a mistake never tried anything new."

–ALBERT EINSTEIN

In a society that often prizes perfection and fears error, this statement is a refreshing reminder that mistakes are not only natural but necessary for growth and progress. When individuals step out of their comfort zones to explore uncharted territories, they inevitably encounter obstacles and setbacks. These experiences, however, are invaluable as they provide critical lessons and insights that cannot be gleaned from success alone. Mistakes push us to rethink, reassess and refine our approaches, ultimately leading to more robust and creative solutions.

Furthermore, this quote underscores the courage required to venture into the unknown. Trying something new often involves a degree of risk and uncertainty, which can be daunting. Yet, it is through taking these risks that we discover new possibilities and expand our horizons. His acknowledgment of the role of mistakes in innovation serves as an encouragement to anyone striving to achieve something meaningful.

Embracing mistakes as a natural part of the journey fosters a growth mindset and resilience. It encourages us to view challenges not as insurmountable barriers but as opportunities for learning and improvement. By understanding that errors are not the antithesis of success but rather a stepping stone towards it, we can cultivate a more adventurous spirit and a more profound sense of creativity and innovation in our personal and professional lives.

Inspiration by Misti Mazurik, Author and Director of Operations at RHG Media Productions

15.

Thought for the Day

"Learn how to be happy with what you have while you pursue all that you want."

–JIM ROHN

16.

Celebrate You

"In a society that profits from your self-doubt, liking yourself is a rebellious act."

–MONEEKA SAWYER, THE BLISSFUL REBEL

In a world filled with social media filters and polished personas, it's easy to get caught up in the comparison game. We struggle to fit into molds crafted by societal standards, all while swimming in a sea of self-doubt.

Every time you find yourself scrolling through an endless feed of curated lives, you're bombarded by messages that silently whisper, "You're not enough." These messages can make it hard to appreciate your unique self. But choosing to like yourself—in all your beautifully imperfect and perfect glory—is like waving a giant flag of rebellion. It's a statement that says you're not going to be bound by other people's views of beauty, success or worth.

When you embrace self-love, you're going against the grain. You're saying, "I am worthy, and I deserve love—especially from myself." In a society that profits from our insecurities, nurturing a relationship with your true self becomes revolutionary.

So, take a moment today to celebrate who you are. Start by looking in a mirror five times today and exclaiming, "Wow! You are beautiful!" Giggle, cringe, react in whatever way you must. But don't back down! Your self-acceptance isn't just an act of love; it's an act of defiance. And the world needs more of that courage.

Inspiration by Moneeka Sawyer-The Blissful Rebel

17.

Thought for the Day

"Vision without action is merely a dream. Action without vision just passes the time. Vision with action can change the world."

–JOEL A. BARKER

18.

Wisdom Unveiled: Empowering Change Starts from Within

Wisdom, the embodiment of life's experiences and lessons, is not merely a possession to be held but a gift to be shared. In the hustle of our busy lives, we often find ourselves disconnected from the profound universe of ancient wisdom that resides within each of us. Until our energetic vibrations and frequencies are aligned to receive our inner wisdom, it remains elusive.

To connect with our wisdom, we must first still the clamor of our minds and become present in the space of the unknown. In the spaciousness of this inner sanctuary, we can hear the whispers of ancient truths and timeless insights. This collective wisdom of the universe, a timeless repository of knowledge, is waiting to be tapped into.

In presence and silence, the secrets of the universe are revealed, not through external seeking, but through internal listening. From this sacred space, we emerge empowered, ready to embody our truth and share it with the world. By living authentically, in alignment with our inner wisdom, we become beacons of light, illuminating awareness of the importance of living your truth.

In the words of Lao Tzu, "When you are content to be simply yourself and don't compare or compete, everyone will respect you." Accessing our wisdom not only allows us to find peace within ourselves but also enables us to offer guidance and support to others in their journey of transformation.

Inspiration by Deborah Wiener, creator of The Energetic Business Feng Shui System™

19.

Wind

Dear one, we invite you to come and dance in the wind. Dance in the storm. Dance in the shelter of our branches. Note our leaves/needles/branches as they move in sync with the wind. A beautifully choreographed dance. Joy, freedom, love, celebration, all in the movement of our branches. Join us in the dance.

You too can dance in the wind; move in sync and flow in life...even in the wind and storms of life. Let them blow movement, fresh air and perspective into your spirit and limbs as you choose to embrace the dance of life. Come dance with us.

Inspiration by The Trees, from The Book Collective

20.

Thought for the Day

If you set goals and go after them with all the determination you can muster, your gifts will take you places that will amaze you.

–LES BROWN

21.

Are You Nourishing Yourself?

Think for a moment about how you are pouring yourself into others—your clients, team members, family, friends, community. Celebrate how wonderful that is!

And then, think about these questions: **Are you letting other things be the priorities versus letting yourself to be poured into? Are you saying yes to things that feel draining rather than nourishing?**

It's so easy to let ourselves fill our days, say we're "too busy," but keep doing those things and adding more while never checking off all the items on our to-do list.

We love serving others, love to say "yes" and we risk losing ourselves in the process. We are so good at continuing to add things to our plates that we occasionally need to **stop. Pause. Evaluate.** This halfway point in the year is a perfect time to do just that:

1. Take just one minute to write down all the things that are on your plate right now—the things you're doing, you're committed to doing and getting ready for.

2. Read the list, noticing what feels pressured and what doesn't. Notice where you're being pulled and where you "need to" (or should or have to) take care of things.

3. Take a good look at the list. You want to make sure that you are making choices that are on purpose for you. Remember, you can choose to say no and take things off this list.

Do you still choose all that is on your list?

Inspiration by Rebecca Hall Gruyter, Influencer, Publisher and Animal Communicator

22.

Thought for the Day

"Many of life's failures are people who did not realize how close they were to success when they gave up."

–THOMAS A. EDISON

23.

Thought for the Day

"Do all the good you can, for all the people you can, in all the ways you can, as long as you can."

–HILLARY CLINTON

24.

Thought for the Day

"The pessimist sees difficulty in every opportunity. The optimist sees opportunity in every difficulty."

–WINSTON CHURCHILL

25.

Surrender–Falling into Balance

A delicious crispness in the air . . . September! Embrace its sacred invitation to the art of balance.

Because let's be real, we've all swung a little too far into the hustle and burned our candles at both ends. Or maybe we've been on the opposite end of the spectrum and slipped into a cozy cocoon of comfort until we feel, well, a little stagnant.

It's a time to let go of any extreme we've been clinging to and bask in the beauty of equilibrium instead as we watch autumn leaves make their graceful descent. Release what needs releasing: self-imposed pressures, the fear of missing out, the constant striving. Let it all flutter away on the crisp autumn breeze.

Open your arms wide to welcome in all the nourishment your soul needs: rest, play, creative expression, quality time with loved ones. Find that exquisite balance between doing and being, ambition and inner peace.

You, my dear friend, are a masterpiece crafted in the image of the Greatest Artist. And like any breathtaking work of art, you are meant to be appreciated from every angle-the passion-fueled energy and the serene, centered calm.

Go ahead and surrender to September's siren song of balance. Let this month be your canvas, and you the brilliant painter finding just the right brushstrokes of vibrance and stillness. Your brilliance was never meant to burn out in a blaze of glory; it was crafted to shine on, eternal and radiant, in perfect harmony.

Inspiration by Janet Bernice Cheney, life-coach and best-selling author

26.

Thought for the Day

"The only way to make sense out of change is to plunge into it, move with it, and join the dance."

–ALAN WATTS

27.

Thought for the Day

"Always strive to do the right thing even when it isn't a popular choice. By doing so, you become a better person."

–TORRON-LEE DEWAR

28.

Delegate

Are you looking to expand and have a bigger impact on your business? It's not something that can be done on your own. When I am at a growth point in my business, I think of my garden—the mint, specifically. It's so beautiful, aromatic and yummy in a glass of iced tea. Yet, if I'm not careful, it starts to take over my whole yard!

In my business, it's the point at which my tasks and responsibilities seem to be taking over everything and smothering new opportunities and projects like the mint in my garden crowding out other blooms. It's time to delegate. **Here are some tips to get started:**

1. List the things you need support on and what you would love to hand over and delegate to someone.

2. If you have a budget to work with, prioritize the work you need to have done and find the people with expertise to do it. Get creative— there are many ways to outsource talent!

3. Consider trading services—as long as it makes sense for your business and is serving both parties. If you choose to make trades, evaluate them regularly to make sure they are a win-win.

4. Make these choices sooner than later—*before* your yard is taken over by mint!

What can you start to delegate today to grow your business, impact and reach?

Inspiration by Rebecca Hall Gruyter, Influencer, Publisher and Animal Communicator

29.

Thought for the Day

"We must believe that we are gifted for something, and that this thing, at whatever cost, must be attained."

–MARIE CURIE

30.

Step Into Your Visibility

My work is about helping experts overcome fear so they can bring their message forward to help the world be a better place. Here are three ways to make this shift to being more visible:

1. **Be *willing* to be seen.** We must be willing to be seen on the same level that we are to serve. In other words, if we want to serve, we must allow others to get to know who we are and how we can serve them. You can't help them if they can't see and hear you.

2. ***Dance with* the fear.** Fear is an emotion that rises when you are stepping into a new space, and your body isn't sure if it's safe yet. Your fear is trying to protect you. In truth, you are not in danger, so you can assure your emotions that what you are feeling is discomfort simply because you are doing something that you haven't ever done before and been willing to feel the emotion and step forward anyway.

3. **Remember your "why"**—the reason you are stepping forward into visibility is to serve more people, to meet a need in the world that you are uniquely qualified and called to do. Your why will always be there to inspire and motivate you to step forward powerfully, even when you're afraid.

I can't wait to see you shine!

Inspiration by Rebecca Hall Gruyter, Influencer and Empowerment leader

October

1.

Remember Who You Are

Remember who you are, remember your birthright, remember the quickening of your spirit when you're in joy and in alignment. There's real power in that. When we step into remembering who we are, there's a strength about it that we can feel that helps us feel grounded in those times when we feel pulled in all directions or taking care of others and forgetting to pay attention to ourselves.

Let's take it a step further. Throughout these days and weeks, tap into this powerful awareness and put out your antenna to tune into noticing:

"What is more of who I am?"

"What am I being called to bring forth?"

When you ask these questions, know that the answer is inside you, waiting to respond. It sometimes is just about tuning in and remembering because you knew it all along. I encourage you to actively look out for that and be prepared for some exciting, clarifying answers to help you step forward.

When we're willing to strip that away and say, "This is me," we find our energy increases, and people really lean in and connect.

Inspiration by Rebecca Hall Gruyter, Influencer, Publisher and Animal Communicator

2.

Thought for the Day

"You can overcome whatever is going on around you if you believe in the light that lives within you."

–JUSTINE EDWARD

3.

Pumpkin(g), Hear me ROAR!

I am Pumpkin(g) When I first met my family at about six months old, I shared my name was Pumpkin. When I joined my family at eight months old, my mom would hold me and sing to me.

When she would sing to me with love in her heart, she made me feel brave like a King. That is what I heard when she sang my name . . . PumpKING. Now, I tap into my King power/energy whenever I want. Especially whenever I am afraid . . . in the King space/energy, I feel her love and become courageous and strong.

What name, song or feeling helps you feel courageous and strong? Hold it in your heart and ROAR!

Inspiration by Pumpkin(g), the cat

4.

Thought for the Day

"The purpose of our lives is to be happy."

–DALAI LAMA

5.

Positivity Is THE Option

"If you're not positive energy, you're negative energy."

–MARK CUBAN

Mark Cuban's quote is a profound perspective on the influence of attitude and mindset in personal and professional realms. By framing energy in binary terms, Cuban underscores the significance of maintaining a positive outlook. Positive energy often manifests as enthusiasm, optimism and proactive behavior, fostering an environment conducive to creativity, collaboration and resilience. In contrast, negative energy, characterized by pessimism, complacency and negativity, can stifle innovation, undermine team spirit and create toxic workspaces.

Cuban's assertion challenges individuals to consciously evaluate and regulate their energy contributions. It implies that neutrality is not an option; one must actively choose to be a force of positivity. This mindset encourages self-awareness and responsibility, urging people to become catalysts for constructive change. In workplaces, positive energy can enhance productivity and morale, motivating teams to achieve common goals and surmount obstacles. On a personal level, it can lead to improved mental health, stronger relationships and greater fulfillment.

However, it is essential to acknowledge that exhibiting positive energy does not mean ignoring challenges or suppressing negative emotions. Instead, it involves adopting a solution-oriented approach, viewing setbacks as opportunities for growth, and encouraging others to do the same. This above quote serves as a powerful reminder of the transformative power of attitude and the enduring impact of our energy on the world around us. What energy are you choosing to bring forward?

Inspiration by Misti Mazurik, Author and Director of Operations at RHG Media Productions

314 | WISDOM FROM THE HEART

6.

Embracing Heartfelt Emotions for Transformation

Feeling your emotions is essential to transformation. You may find yourself numbing your emotions with food, shopping, alcohol, busyness or scrolling mindlessly. It's tempting to distract ourselves from feeling our emotions. The danger of this distraction is that we stay stuck in numbness where energy cannot flow.

One rainy afternoon, I found myself overwhelmed by a flood of emotions. Instead of turning away, I sat in stillness with them, allowing each feeling to wash over me like a gentle shower. As I embraced the storm within, I realized that acknowledging emotions is the first step towards healing. Like a garden watered by tears, our hearts flourish when we allow ourselves to feel deeply.

Feeling holds the key to unlocking your creativity and the manifestation of abundance, prosperity and success. It's the essential conduit to the awareness needed to connect with our intuition. By embracing our emotions, we activate the laws of attraction, aligning our vibrations and frequencies with the energetic flow of the universe.

Stillness provides a gateway to our hearts, inviting spaciousness and the embrace of the unknown. As we surrender to any painful feelings, resistance or fears, we acknowledge their impermanence. Transformation arises from feeling all emotions, releasing them and replacing them with compassion, love and forgiveness. Remember, each emotion is but a passing visitor on the journey to our highest selves. I urge you to dive fearlessly into the ocean of your heart space and have the courage to feel deeply.

Inspiration by Deborah Wiener, creator of The Energetic Business Feng Shui System™

7.

Intuition

The definition of intuition is the ability to understand, feel or know something without needing to think about it or use conscious reasoning.

We have all experienced this. Intuition is that feeling in your gut when you instinctively know that something you are doing is right or wrong. Or something that doesn't feel right. It's that moment when you sense emotion in others. You might not know why you feel that way, but it's always there.

We all have an inner voice, our personal whisper from

the universe . . .

All we have to do is listen.

What is your inner voice saying to you?

Inspiration by Jaimie Harnagel, Shaman

8.

Thought for the Day

"Mediocrity will never do. You are capable of something better."

–GORDON B. HINCKLEY

9.

Success

I spent many years (too many) trying to follow someone else's definition of success because I didn't have my own. I don't anymore because I've explored and **discovered my own definition of success.**

If we don't have clarity on our definition of success (personal, business and financial), we frequently end up following someone else's by default because we don't have our own. I find this to be a big mistake that leads to chasing down dreams that are not your own. And this almost always leads to disillusionment, discouragement and burnout. Do you know your definition of success?

Your definition of success is as personalized as your wardrobe, furniture and what's in your refrigerator! It's easy to think about how the "grass is greener on the other side" for that person whose dream we think we want to follow. But we're only looking at part of the picture (the one we want to believe), and we don't really know what's going on behind the scenes for these people. So, it becomes chasing rainbows.

Take some time to do this simple yet powerful exercise. Ask yourself: **How do I define success in my life, my business [or another aspect in your life that's important to you]?** Have that deep conversation about where you are now, where you want to go and how you want to get there. Get some clarity on what it would look like to live a life and have a business that is meaningful to *you*!

Inspiration by Rebecca Hall Gruyter, Influencer, Publisher and Animal Communicator

10.

Thought for the Day

"Hardships often prepare ordinary people for an extraordinary destiny."

–C.S. LEWIS

11.

Take a Stand for Moving Forward

I've been seeing people bump up against their boundaries during tumultuous times, buffeted back and forth by worry, fear and constant news of disaster and scarcity. They give in to the negativity they feel all around them and shrink back in their businesses and lives.

Their boundaries around their values, ambitions and goals become blurred by other people's messages of fear about the future.

When we put our energy into those fears, more fear is created. We then keep on attracting the same, and we continue to shrink and contract instead of expanding, creating new opportunities and sharing ourselves out into the world. We make small decisions, afraid to struggle and to take risks that will support us in following our dreams once the stormy clouds have parted.

It lights a fire in my belly, a passion that has me stand up and shout, "No! I am not willing to entertain negativity and fear! I am holding strong to my boundaries, taking a stand for *moving forward.*" I know that it's hard, but I believe that we cannot allow difficult times to have us shrink back. We are in this together, and **the world needs us most when the challenges are greatest.**

When I see colleagues and clients allow fear to cause them to drop new projects, slash prices, pause their future plans and strategies, what I truly see is that they are dimming their bright light to shine the path for others.

Choose hope and truth instead of fear and move forward!

Inspiration by Rebecca Hall Gruyter, Influencer and Empowerment Leader

12.

Thought for the Day

"God has made you just the way you are to impact others right where he's placed you."

–TIM HILLER

13.

Thought for the Day

"Fearlessness is like a muscle. I know from my own life that the more I exercise it the more natural it becomes to not let my fears run me."

–ARIANNA HUFFINGTON

14.

Today

"Don't let your past steal your future. Let today be a new beginning."

–MONEEKA SAWYER, THE BLISSFUL MILLIONAIRE

Do you find yourself constantly dwelling on the mistakes or failures of the past? Are you allowing your past experiences to dictate your way of thinking and holding you back from moving forward? It's time to break free from the chains of yesterday and embrace the endless possibilities that today has to offer.

Each new day is a blank canvas waiting to be painted with your dreams and aspirations. Instead of being weighed down by regrets or missed opportunities, use your past experiences as lessons learned to guide you towards a brighter future. Recognize that every moment is a chance to start anew, to redefine yourself and to create a tomorrow that is filled with hope and excitement.

So, don't let yesterday steal your joy. Instead, seize the opportunity that today presents and let it be the start of a new chapter in your journey. Treat today like a blank canvas waiting to be filled with new adventures, opportunities and dreams. Seize the day with enthusiasm and courage, knowing that every step you take is leading you towards a brighter future. Write down a new adventure you would like to take but have been too afraid to take up until now. Let go of the past and embrace the present moment as a chance to create a future that is filled with hope, joy and success. Today is your chance to start anew!

Inspiration by Moneeka Sawyer, the Blissful Millionaire

15.

Thought for the Day

"In order to succeed you must fail, so that you know what not to do the next time."

–ANTHONY J. D'ANGELO

16.

Why Visibility Is Important

"If they cannot see you, if then they cannot hear you, then you cannot help them."

–REBECCA HALL GRUYTER

Visibility is about being seen so that we can shine our light to help others along their path. Let's be easy to find.

I was once *very* resistant to being seen—staying invisible was part of my DNA on a cellular level; it was so programmed into me. When I had to be in front of people, I would shake, turn purple, lose my words and barely be able to say my name! So it was a really long journey to be able to come through that to live and serve in the way that I do today.

I learned that any of the discomforts I might be experiencing was so worth it. If I could make a difference for one other person, to somehow make the path a little bit easier for someone else, then I was willing to be uncomfortable, to stretch outside of my comfort zone, to be vulnerable and imperfect.

To this day, that is still what pulls me forward. I believe that if we tap into our why—to know our purpose, our passion, what we are called to do—it will pull us forward to stretch and succeed on a higher level and *shine* our unique light on the world! What is your why? Will you choose to **shine**?

Inspiration by Rebecca Hall Gruyter, Influencer, Publisher and Animal Communicator

17.

Thought for the Day

"As a man thinketh, so he is."

‒NAPOLEON HILL

18.

Thought for the Day

"When I was 5 years old, my mother always told me that happiness was the key to life. When I went to school, they asked me what I wanted to be when I grew up. I wrote down 'happy'. They told me I didn't understand the assignment, and I told them they didn't understand life."

–JOHN LENNON

19.

Where Are You Showing Up?
Where Are You Shrinking Back?

I often tell my clients how important it is to just *show up* in our imperfect perfections, just where we are in this moment. It is not always easy, as there are going to be times when we want to shrink back instead of showing up.

It can be easy to join something—a networking community, social media group or online group program—with enthusiasm, then you find yourself missing meetings, not responding and not following up with connections. Has that ever happened to you? If so, I encourage you to:

1. **Check-in** on where you are with something you have joined; explore where you are showing up and where you have been shrinking back. Notice with curiosity and explore why.

2. **Take a good look to decide if this is the right fit now.** Your time and energy are precious, your gifts are precious and the world is waiting to receive them. If it doesn't feel in alignment anymore, then make the preparations to leave. Sometimes things are just for a season.

3. **If you decide to continue with the experience,** celebrate and explore ways that you can lean in and enjoy, give and receive even more.

Realize that the world misses out on your contribution when you shrink back. This is why you want to really find those things of value to you that nourish you to *bloom*, support you on an ongoing basis and for which you can make the commitment to show up, contribute and *shine*.

Inspiration by Rebecca Hall Gruyter, Influencer, Publisher and Animal Communicator

20.

Thought for the Day

"When everything seems to be going against you, remember that the airplane takes off against the wind, not with it."

−HENRY FORD

21.

Thought for the Day

"Resilient people do not bounce back from hard experiences; they find healthy ways to integrate them into their lives.... people find that great calamity met with great spirit can create great strength."

–DAVID SCHROEDER

22.

Thought for the Day

"Believe that your life is not ordinary and never look down on what you can do to impact a life."

–SUNDAY ADELAJA

23.

Thought for the Day

"Too many of us are not living our dreams because we are living our fears."

–LES BROWN

24.

Thought for the Day

"In tough times will you whine or shine?"

–DAREN MARTIN

25.

Kindness Ninja

I heard of a teaching strategy that encourages kids to be kind and more importantly, the impact it has. It is creatively called "Kindness Ninja." This is a sneaky way of doing random acts of kindness without the recipient knowing who did the kind deed. What kid doesn't love to be sneaky?! So, my question is, why should the kids get to have all the fun?

During the month of October, let's wear the mask of the Kindness Ninja and see how stealthy we can be with random and unabridged acts of kindness.

Buy a cup of coffee or tea for the next person in the line or bring in a neighbor's trashcans.

A Kindness Ninja can sneak unsuspecting friends trinkets or treasures they want without them knowing it was you. An unsigned card in the mail can brighten anybody's day immeasurably. In this day and age, I think perhaps it's the gesture that someone took the time to do something so personal.

Let's see how many ways we can spread kindness. For that matter, why can't we don this Kindness Ninja warrior costume year-round?

Inspiration by Jaimie Harnagel, Shaman

26.

Thought for the Day

"Our greatest fear should not be of failure but of succeeding at things in life that don't really matter."

–FRANCIS CHAN

27.

Thought for the Day

"My mission in life is not merely to survive, but to thrive; and to do so with some passion, some compassion, some humor, and some style"

–MAYA ANGELOU

28.

Thought for the Day

"October is the treasure of the year, and all the months pay bounty to her store..."

–PAUL LAURENCE DUNBAR

29.

Choose What Matters Most

Do you let yourself be poured into the things that help, nourish and support you to **shine**?

Or are you letting other things, perhaps other people's priorities, become your priority? It's so easy to get "too busy," become overwhelmed and not be able to complete the priorities we set for that day. Does this sound familiar to you?

Part of the challenge is that we are so good at continuing to add things to our plate! We're talented, we want to give and to serve and we want to say "yes" to so many things and people.

This is a good time to stop and check-in.

1. **Take just thirty seconds.** Write down what you currently have on your plate. Make a list of what you have now, what's coming up, what needs to be finished and what needs to be started.

2. **Now, look at your list and notice**: What feels heavy? What feels pressured? What doesn't? It's good to know where you are feeling pulled or depleted instead of feeling poured into.

3. **Reset your "shoulds."** It is very disempowering to say, "I have to, I should, I need to . . ." If you find yourself thinking those words, shift it to "I choose."

4. Now choose what matters most to help you move forward. We can get caught up in doing lots of things and forget to choose to do the most important ones to help us move forward on our goals.

Because, in reality, you are choosing all the time. **You are empowered with the choice to do the things that serve you and let you shine ever brighter. Choose to *shine* and fully share the gift of you!**

Inspiration by Rebecca Hall Gruyter, Influencer, Publisher and Animal Communicator

30.

Thought for the Day

"When life gets you down do you wanna know what you've gotta do? Just keep swimming!"

–DORY, FINDING NEMO

31.

Unmask Your Brilliance

Radiant friend, can you feel that delicious October chill? It's like the universe itself is whispering, "Time to shed what's holding you back and let your true self shine."

In other words, it's time to take off those masks that life sometimes makes us wear. You know what I mean, the "I've got it all together" facade when really our life feels like a beautiful mess. Or the "everything's fine" smile we paste on to hide the doubts and fears that gnaw at us.

Well, this October, here's a challenge: Let's ditch the masquerade and start living as our most authentic, brilliant selves instead! Imagine how freeing it would feel to finally unmask that inner light you've been dimming, that extraordinary spark you were born to share with the world.

Of course, peeling back those layers might feel a little scary at first. Vulnerability has a way of making us feel deliciously unguarded. But here's the thing-you are a breathtaking masterpiece never meant to be hidden away, crafted by the Great Artist.

So go ahead and strip off that false front. Embrace your quirks and contradictions, your messy brilliance and radiant flaws. Let the "real you" take center stage at last, flaws and all, and watch how the world lights up in response to your authenticity.

This October, it's time to unmask your most vibrant self and let that inner radiance blaze bright for all to see. You've got this, dazzle on with your brilliant self!

Inspiration by Janet Bernice Cheney, life-coach and best-selling author

November

1.

Choose Happiness

"Happiness is a choice that requires effort at times."

–AESCHYLUS

This quote captures a deep truth about the human experience. It implies that while happiness is available to all, it is not always a spontaneous or effortless state. Rather, it often demands conscious effort and intentional actions. Life inevitably presents challenges, obstacles and moments of hardship that can diminish our sense of well-being. Nonetheless, the decision to maintain happiness in the face of these struggles speaks to our resilience and determination.

Choosing happiness may involve developing a positive mindset, practicing gratitude or engaging in activities that bring joy and fulfillment. It may require letting go of negativity, forgiving past grievances or seeking supportive relationships. This proactive approach highlights the dynamic nature of happiness; it is not a fixed destination but an ongoing journey. By recognizing that happiness requires effort, we empower ourselves to take charge of our emotional state instead of being passive victims of our circumstances.

Moreover, this viewpoint aligns with various psychological theories that stress the importance of personal agency in attaining well-being. Research in positive psychology supports the notion that individuals can boost their happiness through intentional practices such as mindfulness, kindness and setting meaningful goals. Therefore, Aeschylus' quote remains a timeless reminder that while happiness may not always be easily attained, the effort we invest in cultivating it is undeniably rewarding, leading to a more fulfilling and enriched life.

Inspiration by Misti Mazurik, Author and Director of Operations at RHG Media Productions

2.

*"Don't wait until the fourth Thursday in November,
to sit with family and friends to give thanks.
Make every day a day of Thanksgiving!"*

–CHARMAINE J. FORDE

3.

Wired to Serve

Moving forward on your mission doesn't always mean saying *yes* to every opportunity. You have a choice at any time to say *no*—or even better—*not yet*.

When I say *yes* to something, I know I'm saying *no* to something else I may not even know about yet.

Think about that for a moment. This means that with each opportunity that comes my way, I really want to make sure that **it is the way I am called to serve at the highest level**. And there is no one way to do this; it varies with the type of people we are as well as where we are in our life's journey. We are all wired differently.

We can serve our whole lives in important, fulfilling ways without trying to fit ourselves into a box that isn't in alignment with who we are, who we want to be or what we value.

What I have found is that **you must be willing to be seen on the same level that you want to serve.** If they can't see us, then we can't help those we are called to serve. Discover where your people are and go to them. Be on the platforms they are on, the events they are at and the circles in which they participate.

Inspiration by Rebecca Hall Gruyter, Influencer, Publisher and Animal Communicator

4.

Perspective

Sometimes you just need time to process and <u>be</u>, instead of "do." Don't force things. Release the stress of always trying to make things happen. Take some time for silence. Let the uncontrollable world flow. Step back and <u>allow.</u>

That is equally, if not, more important.

Inspiration by Jaimie Harnagel, Shaman

5.

Thought for the Day

*"Gratitude is a quality similar to electricity:
It must be produced and discharged and
used up in order to exist at all."*

–WILLIAM FAULKNER

6.

Navigating Manifestation with Courage

Your future is not predetermined; it's a blank canvas eagerly awaiting your touch of alchemy, your spark of magic. The universe responds to the energy you emit; like attracts like.

As Anais Nin said, "Life shrinks or expands in proportion to one's courage." Along the way, we will need to be courageous in facing anything blocking our path to manifestation. We need to identify our fears, for fear is merely a trickster, drawing more of what you fear into your reality.

You may find yourself playing small, using survival tactics to stay safe but stifling growth. Erecting walls around your heart only serves to block the flow of energy, hindering the path to manifestation.

Sit in stillness and reflection to realize the power you hold within. With courage, dismantle those walls and embrace vulnerability as your strength. It's within the depths of surrender that true manifestation thrives, birthing miracles beyond your imagination.

With each stride forward, attune yourself to the dynamic currents of manifestation swirling around you to reveal the full spectrum of your manifestation potential. Journey forward with courage and openness, allowing your wisdom and spaciousness to light the way.

Remember as Eleanor Roosevelt shared, "The future belongs to those who believe in the beauty of their dreams!"

Inspiration by Deborah Wiener, creator of The Energetic Business Feng Shui System™

7.

Thought for the Day

"Love the giver more than the gift."

–BRIGHAM YOUNG

8.

Being in Service

"All that is not given, is lost."

−HASARI PAL

Inherently, a quote I live by. We may think we are here to grow up, get a job, start a family and move through the business of life, but on a higher level, we are really here to be in service of others. There is no greater purpose.

At the same time, serving and lifting up others reveals the best version of ourselves.

How can you be of service today?

Inspiration by Jaimie Harnagel, Shaman

9.

Gratitude's Gentle Embrace

Hello to the familiar brisk November chill! It's like the world is extending a hurry-up and get warm, cozy invitation to come home-to ourselves, to each other and to the radiant light within.

It's true, we've all had those seasons where we've gotten a little lost, right? Wandering aimlessly down detours of bitterness, regret or self-doubt until we've forgotten our way back to our genuine selves. But in the stillness of this sacred month, we're reminded that the path home has been there all along, paved with the twin graces of gratitude and forgiveness.

So go ahead and let November's crisp breezes blow away the cobwebs. Take stock of all the blessings that surround you, from the tiniest miracle to the most breathtaking wonder. Let each one fill your heart with a renewed sense of awe and appreciation for your precious life.

And where you've strayed into darkness or disconnection, let your inner courage bring you to forgiveness-to others, of course, but more importantly, to yourself. You are an exquisite masterpiece worthy of infinite compassion and grace.

Let yourself release old grudges, self-criticism and the heaviness that's been weighing you down. Let it all go with an open-hearted exhale, leaving you delightfully free to embrace all the beauty that awaits.

This November, come home to the vibrant, grateful, forgiving soul you were born to be. Let gratitude's gentle embrace surround you, and step forward into the radiant light of your most authentic self.

Inspiration by Janet Bernice Cheney, life-coach and best-selling author

10.

Thought for the Day

"Turn your wounds into wisdom."

–OPRAH WINFREY

11.

Take the Stage!

Many powerful experts with valuable information, unfortunately, have difficulty finding and getting on stages (virtual as well as live), in front of the people who would most benefit from their knowledge and gifts.

<u>Here are three keys to success that I've learned along the way:</u>

1. **Know there are stages available to you.** Community leaders with speaking opportunities want great speakers for their audiences as badly as you want the chance to speak.

2. **Know what stages are right for you.** Take some time to identify and focus on the opportunities that are best for you, for example, your ideal audience, the size of the audience (especially if you're new to speaking), and if the host's concept of the experience is aligned with yours.

3. **Connect from a place of service.** Make sure to cultivate the spirit of service within yourself first before connecting with an opportunity—try seeing the world through the eyes of the person with whom you're trying to connect: what are they looking for? What are they most excited about? What solutions are they seeking for their people?

Know that the world needs the unique and wonderful gifts you bring. So, take the stage and *shine*!

Inspiration by Rebecca Hall Gruyter, Influencer, Publisher and Animal Communicator

12.

Your Heart Is Waiting

"In every heartbeat of the Bliss Revolution lies a spark—an invitation to awaken joy, embrace compassion and realize that true transformation begins within."

–MONEEKA SAWYER, THE BLISSFUL REBEL

Have you ever stopped to feel your heartbeat? It's amazing, isn't it? The truth is, in every heartbeat, there lies an invitation—an invitation to awaken the joy that lives inside of you.

When we talk about transformation, it's easy to look outward, expecting change to come from external circumstances. But what if the most profound changes start from within us? The Bliss Revolution urges us to explore this inner landscape and reconnect with joy that may have been dulled by life's challenges. Embracing our compassionate selves is not just a personal journey; it radiates outward, encouraging others to reflect that kindness back.

Imagine a world where every heartbeat vibrates with joy and compassion! We can inspire that change simply by nurturing our inner bliss. It begins with small things—a kind gesture, a gentle word or taking a moment to appreciate ourselves.

Ultimately, let us remember, true transformation begins from within. Together, let's heed the call of the Bliss Revolution. Awaken that spark; let it lead you to a more joyful, compassionate life. Your heart is waiting.

Inspiration by Moneeka Sawyer-The Blissful Rebel

13.

Thought for the Day

"Reflect upon your present blessings—of which every man has many—not on your past misfortunes, of which all men have some."

–CHARLES DICKENS

14.

Thought for the Day

"Remember no one can make you feel inferior without your consent."

–ELEANOR ROOSEVELT

15.

Thought for the Day

"Wear gratitude like a cloak, and it will feed every corner of your life."

–RUMI

16.

Make a Joyful Noise

My mom says I am quite verbal. I have a loud meow/voice that carries. I cry out in joy, in play, to warn, or for attention and in connection. I have lots to say and appreciate people/others hearing me, talking with me and being with me. I bet you have lots to say too . . . what joyful noise can you make? That can carry your love, vibration and important messages to others?

Share your voice and let your message(s) be heard. MEOW! I know others are waiting to hear all that you have to share.

Inspiration by Pumpkin(g), the cat

17.

Thought for the Day

"Your need for acceptance can make you invisible in this world. Don't let anything stand in the way of the light that shines through this form. Risk being seen in all of your glory."

–JIM CARREY

18.

Thought for the Day

"Enjoy the little things, for one day you may look back and realize they were the big things."

–ROBERT BRAULT

19.

It Is a Courageous Act to Say "Yes" to *You*

From a childhood of abuse, I know a lot about being disempowered and how to overcome that in order to step into my passion, power and gifts. The gift I have found is my passion for helping other women step forward and into their courageous and empowered selves, no matter what.

Today I celebrate you for saying "yes" to your journey. I know you have your own stories or messages you have received that have disempowered you in some way. I also know that you are taking the journey to stand up, focus on your purpose and joy and **shine**!

I encourage you not to take this journey alone. **It is also a courageous act to be willing to let others walk beside you** to support and cheer you on in life. I invite you to pause, take a deep breath and be ready to receive the inspiration and wisdom of others who are on this journey with you. We need others to encourage us, to speak wisdom and truth into us, to love us and cheer us on and to help us stand up again when we fall. And to help us stay courageous and continue to say "yes" to ourselves.

Take that in, along with the magical beauty of the season.

Inspiration by Rebecca Hall Gruyter, Influencer, Publisher and Animal Communicator

20.

Crystal Support

Allow us to partner with you, to lend you our beauty, vibrancy, frequency/energy to you. We can help you heal, uplift your energy, clear spaces of negative energy, amplify your work, strengthen your connections, protect and support you.

Today, feel into what you need and look up what crystal can help you with that need. We have evolved over millions of years to powerfully algin with you and the work you are called to do...and all that you are called to be.

Let our love, energy and support in. We love to see you shine your beauty and light into the world.

Inspiration by The Crystalline Council, from The Book Collective

21.

Thought for the Day

*"What you do has far greater
impact than what you say."*

–STEPHEN COVEY

22.

Wonder in Your Life

How special is the wonderment of children—when we don't have any fear and treat all beings the same way, without judgment!

In what ways do you still see wondrous things in your life?

Even as an adult, I like to look for wonder in my life, to see the magic that might present itself to me at any moment. There is a powerful exercise to invite in wonderment and magic by setting your expectations for it.

When you are about to enter a new situation or go to an event, check-in with yourself by asking:

- *What is it that I need to know or have [in this situation or at this event]?*

- *What will encourage me, equip me, empower me to bring in my magic?*

- *What is it that I'm willing to receive in this experience I am about to have?*

Then, open yourself up to connect with the answers. You may find wonder in the most unexpected places!

We are empowered with the choice to hold things in our lives in wonder and awe. We can make decisions about what we will trust and how we will treat each other. We can choose the lens through which we see our world. I hope you choose to see the wonder, love and magic in the world.

Inspiration by Rebecca Hall Gruyter, Influencer, Publisher and Animal Communicator

23.

Thought for the Day

"When you practice gratefulness, there is a sense of respect towards others."

–DALAI LAMA

24.

Thought for the Day

"A thankful receiver bears a plentiful harvest."

–WILLIAM BLAKE

25.

Bliss in Thanksgiving

*"Thanksgiving is not just a day, it's a way
of living in bliss every day."*

–MONEEKA SAWYER, THE BLISSFUL MILLIONAIRE

Thanksgiving is more than just a yearly tradition. It's a mindset, a way of life that can bring joy and gratitude into every day we are alive. Imagine waking up each morning with a heart full of thankfulness and embracing every moment with appreciation for the abundance that surrounds us.

When we live in a state of thanksgiving, we can see the beauty in the simple things, find happiness in unexpected places and connect with others on a deeper level. It's about finding the gift in every situation (good or bad), and recognizing the countless blessings that fill our lives.

Instead of waiting for one day a year to express gratitude, let's make every day a celebration of thanksgiving. Let's smile at the sunrise, savor each meal, cherish the love of our family and friends and take time to appreciate the little miracles that happen all around us.

I urge you to embrace this way of living in bliss every single day. Let gratitude be your guiding light, and watch as your life becomes richer, more meaningful and filled with endless bliss. Today, as you go through your day, write down whatever comes to your mind that you can give thanks for. And as you write it, feel your thanksgiving deep inside your heart. Thanksgiving is not just a day—it's a beautiful way of being.

Inspiration by Moneeka Sawyer, the Blissful Millionaire

26.

Thought for the Day

"Promise me; you will always remember: You're braver than you believe and stronger than you seem, and smarter than you think."

–CHRISTOPHER ROBIN TO WINNIE THE POOH, AS WRITTEN BY A.A. MILNE

27.

Showing Up to Make a Difference

Sometimes the journey to blooming and shining can be uncomfortable and make you feel vulnerable. It can feel easier to say *no* and stay safe than to say *yes* and step up. But consider this: What if by doing that uncomfortable, difficult, scary thing, you made a difference for another person? *Or maybe hundreds or thousands of people?*

That is your potential power of showing up and being willing to be seen, to *shine*! What does it take to be willing? Simply:

- Show up. Say *yes* to those opportunities that pull at your heart. (Don't worry about how to do it; the *how* will almost always come after the commitment of *yes*.)

- Let people support you and cheer you on.

- Share what is on your heart.

- Reach out your hand and make a difference for one person.

What happens when you take this exciting, uncomfortable, scary, joyful journey? People will say, "Thank you. Thank you for shining a light on my path. Thank you for caring enough, loving enough, being enough to reach out your hand to me, for making a difference in my life." That is how we make a global difference, heart to heart, life to life. How can you show up today and reach your hand out to help another?

Inspiration by Rebecca Hall Gruyter, Influencer, Publisher and Animal Communicator

28.

Thought for the Day

"You ought to be thankful a whole heaping lot, for the places and people you're lucky you're not!"

–DR. SEUSS

29.

Happiness

"Bliss is not a destination, but a state of mind found in the beauty of each moment."

–MONEEKA SAWYER, THE BLISSFUL MILLIONAIRE

Often, we find ourselves chasing after external sources of happiness-a dream job, a perfect relationship or material possessions. We believe that once we achieve these goals, we will finally achieve lasting happiness. But the truth is, true bliss is not a place we can arrive at. It is not something external that we can seek out. Instead, it is a state of mind that can be found in the beauty of each moment.

Every moment in life is precious and unique. Whether we are gazing at a breathtaking sunrise, sharing a laugh with a loved one or simply enjoying a quiet moment of solitude, there is beauty to be found if we are willing to see it. It is in these moments that we can experience true bliss-a feeling of peace, contentment and gratitude for the gift of life.

So, today, remember to pause, to slow down and to take the time to appreciate the beauty that surrounds you. Look for the small moments of joy and wonder that are scattered throughout your day. Embrace them fully and let them fill your heart with warmth, gratitude and joy.

Inspiration by Moneeka Sawyer, the Blissful Millionaire

30.

Thought for the Day

"For me, every hour is grace. And I feel gratitude in my heart each time I can meet someone and look at his or her smile."

–ELIE WIESEL

December

1.

Thought for the Day

*"The stars shine a little brighter
when I tell them about you."*

−SIRAPA MALLA

2.

Friendship Pie

When I was young, I had a book that I loved called, *Honey*. Honey, a teenage girl, doesn't get what she needs from her home life so as she makes friends, she "adopts" them as her family. They fill her life with love and happiness and they become a part of her "pie."

I always think of this book when I think of my close circle of friends. I left home at an early age and they became my family, each one teaching me different life lessons and providing support as needed. They taught me so much: how to drive, how to live on my own, how to fix things, even how to wrap presents, etc. I learned through them and from them. Their support was, and still is, immeasurable.

Your family will always be your family. They will (hopefully!) support you and stand by you no matter what differences you may have. However, you can't possibly get everything you need from your parents or a partner. Friends are the family we get to choose. In doing so, we bring in what we need. They fill us up, encourage us, put us back together and they hold our hands. Even new friends can become part of our Tribe.

Honor your friends today. Get in touch with old friends and new. Phone calls, emails, e-cards, even texts are great ways to reach out. See if you can make plans for lunch or a cup of coffee with a friend or even a phone date.

Inspiration by Jaimie Harnagel, Shaman

3.

Thought for the Day

"Don't let the past steal your present. This is the message of Christmas: We are never alone."

–TAYLOR CALDWELL

4.

Be Mindful of What You Feed Yourself

They say you are what you eat, meaning that all of the food you take in can either make your body sicker *or* keep you healthy and fit on a cellular level.

The same is true for what you take in through your mind and spirit. It's important to be mindful of the types of things you let pour into you—the things that you watch, what you listen to, that you're choosing to include. **They become part of your emotional and mental health, part of your very DNA.**

Stop, pause and look at where you are doing the things that matter most to you. Make sure the things you are doing are truly in alignment with what matters most to you to bring forth. Ask **how you are nourishing yourself in ways that keep you in alignment.**

Make it a practice to be aware of what you are taking in and receiving. Invite into your life the things that feed into you—positive media, messaging that will uplift, encourage and empower you.

Like choosing healthy food for your body, choose positive, informative, responsible messages that nourish you, uplift you and help you grow. You're worth it. Be willing to nourish yourself.

Inspiration by Rebecca Hall Gruyter, Influencer, Publisher and Animal Communicator

5.

Thought for the Day

"I find that it's the simple things that remind you of family around the holidays."

–AMY ADAMS

6.

Make Magic During the Holidays

Have you ever experienced this? You host a holiday dinner or party with a lot of people. Your head is filled with all the distractions around the event—the planning, cooking, gifts, attending to guests, family drama, excitement and laughter. Then, it's over. And you hardly remember any part of it!

An event that was supposed to be memorable instead is a blur. Yes, it's happened to me too—I wasn't fully present in the moment, and those precious moments never had a chance to embed on a cellular level.

My holiday gift to you is this: Before you start something or go to an event, take some moments to stop, breathe and ask:

"What is it that I need to know or to have today?"
"What is it that will encourage me, equip me and empower me to bring in my magic?"
"What can I appreciate and celebrate in this moment?"

Taking this a powerful step further, ask yourself: **"What is it that I'm willing to receive?" (Today, in general, or in regard to the activity or event you are about to experience.)** Then open yourself up to connect with the answers. You may be surprised by the magic that happens!

Inspiration by Rebecca Hall Gruyter, Influencer, Publisher and Animal Communicator

7.

Thought for the Day

"December is a month of enormous potential. It's a time when we can all give and receive, a time when the spirit of humanity shines brightest."

–MICHAEL JOSEPHSON

8.

Love Fully

Humans are sometimes afraid to love fully . . . to beam their hearts out into the world. They want love but frequently hold part of their hearts back. But you see that is exactly what the world needs . . . more love. It is time we all choose to love more fully . . . with full hearts. It matters.

Feel the love around you. So much is available to you. As an example, think about the animals in your life, know that they have chosen you, you are their mission and they love you fully and deeply. Feel their love beaming to your heart. Open your hearts and receive. When you pause and go out into nature, see the love all around you and receive it and in turn share/beam your love out fully.

This is how we make the world a more loving place. It starts in the heart.

Inspiration by Pumpkin(g), the cat

9.

Thought for the Day

"Let all your thinks be thanks."

–W.H. AUDEN

10.

Thought for the Day

"If you can tune into your purpose and really align with it, setting goals so that your vision is an expression of that purpose, then life flows much more easily."

–JACK CANFIELD

11.

Keeping Busy in What Brings You Joy

Do you know people who just seem to be everywhere, doing everything effortlessly, with lots of joyful energy? You might find yourself wondering why you can't be like them. You wonder if you are enough. You feel bogged down in tasks facing you that do not feel joyful at all.

I used to do, do, do until I became stressed out and burned out. People thought I was "that person," but in fact, I was definitely missing the joy! Until I learned some important lessons about self-nourishment. Here are practices that have helped me stay joyful and balanced:

1. I find things that bring me joy and having them in my life is non-negotiable. I start every day with routines that give me a boost and keep me centered.

2. If I find that I begin to be that former stressed-out creature, I've learned to pause right there before it gets too far and breathe deeply. (Stress has us breathing too shallowly.)

3. I might take a timeout or a break, doing something that will bring me back to joy.

4. When I am making a decision, I always run it by questions like: Is this going to make the path easier for another? Will this help someone else bloom and share their talents and gifts?

What practices are you building into your daily life to support, center and nourish you?

Inspiration by Rebecca Hall Gruyter, Influencer, Publisher and Animal Communicator

12.

The Art of Harmonious Living: Exploring the Energetic Business Feng Shui System™

Feng Shui, an ancient art of harmonizing natural energies, unveils the pathway to abundance, prosperity and success. The Energetic Business Feng Shui System™ transcends mere physical rearrangement; it's a profound journey of self-transformation using multiple modalities to realign our energetic frequencies towards harmony, balance and fulfillment.

It's about orchestrating a symphony of positive vibrations to resonate with the universe's rhythms. Your thoughts, words and actions paint the canvas of your reality. Transforming the energy you broadcast into the cosmos changes the course of your life, allowing the universe to fulfill your dreams.

Opening your heart to receive requires vulnerability and surrender to allow yourself to receive your gifts. The Energetic Business Feng Shui System™ is about harnessing the law of attraction to cocreate your destiny with the universe. Watch your world transform into a sanctuary of happiness and prosperity.

As you journey through metamorphosis, remember Socrates' wisdom: "The secret to change is to focus all of your energy not on fighting the old, but on building the new."

Inspiration by Deborah Wiener, creator of The Energetic Business Feng Shui System™

13.

Small and Mighty

You can miss me if you hurry by and not even know I was there. But if you slllloooowww down to listen; there is a message I have for your heart today.

There is no one else just like you! You are special and a treasure. Let this message into your heart and with each heart beat feel it echo through all of you...every cell of your body. In this season, remember to share the gift of you with others. Slow down, truly see what is there, be present and enjoy connecting with yourself and others. Listen to the messages of your heart.

Inspiration by Twiggy, the Stick Bug, from The Book Collective

14.

Thought for the Day

"Happiness is there for the taking, and the making."

–OPRAH WINFREY

15.

Broken

*"Broken just means that there are more
pieces to share with the world."*

−MISTI MAZURIK

Imperfections and hardships can lead to greater opportunities for connection and growth. When something breaks, it often reveals hidden layers and facets that were previously unnoticed, each piece telling its own story. Similarly, when a person experiences challenges or setbacks, these moments of "brokenness" can unveil deeper aspects of their character, resilience and empathy. Instead of viewing these fragments as flaws, we can see them as unique contributions to the tapestry of human experience.

Each piece of a broken object can serve a new purpose, finding its way into different lives and settings, much like how our own experiences can touch and inspire others in unexpected ways. This perspective encourages us to embrace our vulnerabilities and share our stories, fostering a sense of community and understanding. It shifts the focus from the notion of being damaged to being multifaceted, each piece reflecting a part of our journey.

Moreover, this idea aligns with the Japanese art of kintsugi, where broken pottery is mended with gold, highlighting the breaks rather than hiding them, and thus celebrating the object's history. Similarly, our own "cracks" can be seen as enhancements that add to our unique beauty and depth. By sharing our pieces with the world, we contribute to a richer, more diverse collective experience. Embracing our brokenness becomes a powerful act of self-acceptance and generosity, allowing us to transform our pain into something meaningful and beautiful.

Inspiration by Misti Mazurik, Author and Director of Operations at RHG Media Productions

16.

Thought for the Day

"May your walls know joy, may every room hold laughter, and every window open to great possibility."

–MARY ANNE RADMACHER

17.

Thought for the Day

"Blessed is the season which engages the whole world in a conspiracy of love."

–HAMILTON WRIGHT MABIE

392 | WISDOM FROM THE HEART

18.

Claim Bliss

"Bliss is not a privilege, it is your birthright.
Claim it with gratitude."

–MONEEKA SAWYER, THE BLISSFUL MILLIONAIRE

In the hustle and bustle of our everyday lives, it's easy to forget that true happiness is not reserved for a lucky few. It is a gift ingrained in each and every one of us. Within each of us lies the innate ability to cultivate joy and embrace the moments of bliss that life has to offer.

How do you claim your birthright of bliss? The secret to doing so lies in the powerful act of gratitude. When we shift our perspective to focus on the blessings and beauty that surround us, we open our hearts to invite in joy and contentment. Gratitude acts as a beacon, guiding us towards the light of happiness that is always within our reach.

Claim your birthright of bliss with an open heart and a grateful spirit. Let gratitude be your compass as you navigate life's ups and downs, and you will find that happiness is not a privilege, but a right that is yours to cherish and enjoy.

Start now, and when you wake up each morning, take a moment to breathe in the fresh air and give thanks for the gift of a new day. Embrace the challenges and triumphs that come your way, knowing that they are opportunities for growth and resilience. Surround yourself with love and positivity, and watch as bliss blossoms within you.

Inspiration by Moneeka Sawyer, the Blissful Millionaire

19.

Thought for the Day

"Never dull your shine for somebody else."

–TYRA BANKS

20.

Unwrapping Appreciation

Hey there, radiant soul! Can you feel that electric December tingle? It's like the whole world is buzzing with anticipation, waiting to be unwrapped and adored.

In the hustle of the season, it's easy to let the little miracles slip by unnoticed. We get so focused on checking tasks off our lists that we forget to pause and truly appreciate the gifts all around us.

For December, unwrap each moment like the precious present it is. No perfection here, just give it a try. Savor the twinkling lights and the loved ones' laughter. Breathe in the scent of fresh-baked cookies and hot cocoa with childlike wonder . . . and, if you're so inclined, get in a Christmas movie or two.

I'll say it again, you are a breathtaking masterpiece from the Great Artist, a walking miracle, meant to be cherished and adored, just the way you are. Go ahead and bask in the magic of each December day, like a kid on Christmas morning.

Let your heart overflow with appreciation for all the beauty around you-the cozy warmth of your home, the quirky traditions that make you smile, the delicious messes and mundane miracles that make this wild life so vibrantly yours.

This month, don't just unwrap presents-unwrap your ability to revel in every blessed moment too. Let that spirit of awe and gratitude spill over into the new year, carrying you forward on a tidal wave of appreciation for the precious journey that is your life.

Inspiration by Janet Bernice Cheney, life-coach and best-selling author

21.

Thought for the Day

"May your walls know joy, may every room hold laughter, and every window open to great possibility"

–MARY ANNE RADMACHER

22.

Small Acts of Kindness

"Join the ranks of the blissful rebels, where every small act of kindness challenges the status quo, proving that love and courage can reshape the world, one quiet moment at a time."

—MONEEKA SAWYER, THE BLISSFUL REBEL

In our world that often glorifies big gestures and loud movements, it's so easy to feel swallowed up by the chaos. But there's profound strength in the concept of being a "blissful rebel." As this quote reminds us, every small act of kindness holds the potential to challenge the status quo. Imagine how powerful it is when we choose to lead with love and courage, even in the tiniest ways.

Think about the last time you smiled at a stranger or held the door open for someone. Those moments may seem minor, but they create ripples. They can make someone's day, uplift spirits and foster connection in our fast-paced lives. Each time we choose kindness over indifference, we quietly resist a culture that sometimes prioritizes self-interest.

We aren't all called to be front-line activists or lead grand movements; most of us can impact our spheres through our everyday choices. It's about embracing the little victories—sharing a thoughtful comment, standing up for someone's voice or just being there with an understanding heart. With each act, however small, we become part of a blissful revolution, shifting perspectives and inspiring others to follow.

So, why not join the ranks of blissful rebels today? What small act of love, kindness or joy can you share to transform your world today?

Inspiration by Moneeka Sawyer–The Blissful Rebel

23.

Thought for the Day

"It's not how much we give but how much love we put into giving."

–MOTHER THERESA

24.

Patches, The Christmas Cat

Is it possible for a little, black-and-white, spotted, furry, twelve-pound being to have an impact on every life he touched?

Yes! That was my Patches. There was something so special about Patches, who joined my life one Christmas as a kitten and stayed with me for seventeen years. He captivated hearts with his spirit, love of others and powerful presence.

Even those who weren't "cat people" were drawn to him. He brought joy, love and peace to all those around him. If a friend came to visit me, upset over something, Patches would come curl up next to them or lie on their lap. It was as if he understood that they needed some extra love in those moments.

People would call me all the time to share how Patches just understood them when they were having a really bad day. They would come and visit him. In fact, in his final days, people stopped by to spend time with him and thank him. They shared their love and presence with him just as he once had with them.

It's no surprise that the Christmas cat left a lasting legacy to me and all the lives and hearts he touched. I miss him but feel his heart and spirit every Christmas, and it makes me smile and feel loved.

Do you have a furry or feathered friend in your life who has left a beautiful legacy to your life? Celebrate the gift they have been and are in your life.

Inspiration by Rebecca Hall Gruyter, Influencer, Publisher and Animal Communicator

25.

Thought for the Day

"Our hearts grow tender with childhood memories and love of kindred, and we are better throughout the year for having, in spirit, become a child again at Christmas-time."

–LAURA INGALLS WILDER

26.

Thought for the Day

"The best and most beautiful things in this world cannot be seen or even heard, but must be felt with the heart."

–HELEN KELLER

27.

Thought for the Day

"Celebrate endings, for they precede new beginnings."

–JONATHAN LOCKWOOD HUIE

28.

Thought for the Day

"There are far better things ahead
than any we leave behind."

–C.S. LEWIS

29.

Aim for the Stars in the New Year!

*"It's not that we aim too high and miss, it's
that we aim too low and hit."*

–LES BROWN

Let's explore how you will shine in the new year. This is the perfect time to look at your future—where are you going, what are you called to be and where are you called to stretch. **I encourage you to aim high and far, aim further than you can even see exactly where it will land!**

Set goals for yourself that scare you a little bit, aren't the safe route or are somewhere you have never been before. You don't have to know the *how*; you can figure that out later. **Look for opportunities to reach for that thing that's so far out there you can hardly believe you're claiming it.** A goal that, if you told people, they wouldn't even know how you are going to reach. You feel a quickening in your spirit and a little bit of terror, but you're going to do it anyway—the sky's the limit!

When we're bringing magic into your life and into others' lives, it takes a willingness to set those goals, a willingness to go where we haven't gone before, to stand out, to *shine*! Aim high!

Inspiration by Rebecca Hall Gruyter, Influencer, Publisher and Animal Communicator

30.

Thought for the Day

"All our dreams can come true, if we have the courage to pursue them."

–WALT DISNEY

31.

Thought for the Day

*"Tomorrow is the first blank page of a
365-page book. Write a good one."*

–BRAD PAISLEY

BY SUBJECT

Abundance/Money
January: 15
April: 15
August: 27

Choice
January: 4, 8, 12, 27, 30
February: 1, 18, 26, 28
March: 18, 21, 26
April: 12, 25, 29
May: 1, 22
June: 5
July: 6, 20, 24, 31
August: 3
September: 21
October: 28, 29
November: 1, 3
December: 6, 18

**Dream/Bring Your
Dreams Forward**
January: 8, 9, 21, 23, 25
February: 1
March: 6
June: 25
July: 11
October: 23
December: 29, 30

**Empowerment/Encouragement/
Inspiration/Hope**
January: 21, 31
February: 5, 11, 20, 22

March: 8, 12, 15
April: 12, 22, 21
May: 26
June: 23
August: 4, 19
September: 3
October: 2, 3, 10, 20, 30
November: 22, 26
December: 1, 13, 16, 30

Energy
February: 19
March: 25
May: 24, 30
July: 5, 9, 13, 17, 20, 27
August: 11, 28
September: 13, 19
October: 5
December: 6, 12

Family/Relationships
February: 3, 7, 14
March: 9, 14
May: 4, 17
June: 4
July: 18
August: 2, 18
September: 5, 9
October: 25
November: 2
December: 2, 5, 22

October: 12, 16, 25, 26
November: 6, 8, 16, 17
December: 10, 12

Stop/Pause/Listen
February: 3
March: 2, 16
June: 3

Success
January: 7, 10, 13
March: 3, 4, 10, 14, 19
April: 6, 7, 8, 14
May: 3
August: 4, 17
September: 14, 22
October: 9, 11, 14, 15, 26
December: 29

Support
January: 21
March: 8, 15
May: 8, 17
June: 2
August: 28
September: 6, 8, 19
November: 20

Transformation/Growth
January: 6, 12
February: 2, 19, 25
April: 10, 28, 30
September: 24, 25, 26
October: 6
November: 12
December: 12

Wonderfully Made/Shine
January: 14
March: 1, 5, 23
April: 1, 18
May: 10, 13
June: 9, 20, 24, 27, 30
July: 1, 4, 12
August: 10, 13
September: 1, 12, 16
October: 31
November: 27
December: 19

LEARN MORE ABOUT
OUR AUTHORS

Janet Bernice Cheney is an international best-selling author and speaker, and John Maxwell-certified life coach. She also volunteers to encourage and educate women rising from trauma and dealing with grief, divorce, loss of a child or domestic violence. A survivor of each of these, along with psychological abuse, she has a deep passion for helping women change their lives. An English instructor for over twenty years to non-traditional and low-income students across the US, she met both online and in person in a university setting. Janet loves to cross-stitch and watch English murder mysteries. She has never lost her crush on Peter O'Toole. Her internationally best-selling book, So *Many Freakin' Secrets*, (2024) is available on Amazon.com.

jbernice60@gmail.com
801-995-1182
https://www.healingyoursecrets.com/
https://www.facebook.com/janetmBer
linkedin.com/in/janet-cheney-310634301
https://x.com/Janet_secrets
www.youtube.com/@janetcheney4300
https://www.instagram.com/jbernice68/

Rebecca Hall Gruyter is a global influencer, a #1 international best-selling author, an animal communicator, a compiler and publisher (helping over one thousand authors become bestsellers), a radio show host (reaching over one million listeners on eight networks), and an empowerment leader. She has built multiple platforms to help experts reach more people. These platforms include radio, podcasts, books, magazines, the Speaker Talent Search, and live events, creating a powerful promotional reach of over ten million!

Rebecca is the CEO of RHG Media Productions, the founder of Your Purpose Driven Practice, and the creator of the Speaker Talent Search. Rebecca has personally contributed to forty-plus published books and multiple magazines, and she has been quoted in major media including *Huffington Post*, ABC, CBS, NBC, Fox, and Thrive Global. Today, she wants you to be seen, be heard, and SHINE!

Email: **Rebecca@YourPurposeDrivenPractice.com**

Websites and Social Media:

http://www.YourPurposeDrivenPractice.com
http://www.RHGTVNetwork.com
http://www.SpeakerTalentSearch.com
https://www.facebook.com/rhallgruyter
https://www.linkedin.com/in/rebecca-hall-gruyter-2802669/
http://www.x.com/Rebeccahgruyter
https://www.instagram.com/rhg_global_community/
http://www.EmpoweringWomenTransformingLives.com
http://www.rebeccahallgruyter.linktoexpert.com/

Jaimie Harnagel is a Crystal Intuitive, Shaman, Reiki Master, Crystal Shop Owner, Animal Communicator and #1 International Best- Selling Author, co-authoring *Step Forward and Shine, Empowering You and Transforming Lives* and *Animal Legacies.* She was also featured in *RHG Magazine.*

When working with any healing modality, she channels her holistic practice of mind, body and spirit into opportunities to lift others up and encourage them to shine. Her mission to encourage and inspire others to share their own beautiful light with the world is strongly threaded through everything she does.

In her downtime, Jaimie enjoys diamond painting, hiking, binge reading and drum circles. She resides in Arizona with her husband and their magical kitty friend, Onyx.

Email address: **bjharnagel@msn.com**
Facebook: **https://www.facebook.com/JaimieHarnagel3**

Misti Mazurik holds a master's degree in political science from California University of Pennsylvania and is a certified teacher. She considers herself to be a Jill of all trades as she has worked in many different fields from sales and marketing to human resources. But her joy is working with authors and her amazing coworkers at RHG Media Productions as the Director of Operations.

She believes to live a positive life is to live a happy and fulfilled life. She incorporates her, "Why did this happen for me?" principle in her everyday life and lives blissfully every day!!

What sparks the most joy for her is her family. Her family includes her husband of eleven years, her three cats, her RHG Media Productions family, as well as the gaming community that she belongs to.

Connect with Misti on LinkedIn: **https://www.linkedin.com/in/misti-mazurik/**

Author and Director of Operations, RHG Media Productions

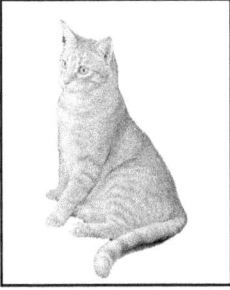

Pumpkin is a two-year-old orange previously feral cat that likes to be called Pumpking. He likes the idea of being in charge and tries to live up to what a good king would do in protecting and taking care of their kingdom. He is diligent about patrolling, protecting and taking care of his home, family and others. He loves his family; and it is important to him to be a good cat. He values family as he knows what it is like to not have a family and to wish for one and try to find one. Pumpking loves with his full heart, has a big personality and is honored and excited to be part of this book. He loves to talk and is excited to share with all that are led to read his inspirations.

He can be reached through Rebecca Hall Gruyter at **Rebecca@ YourPurposeDrivenPractice.com**

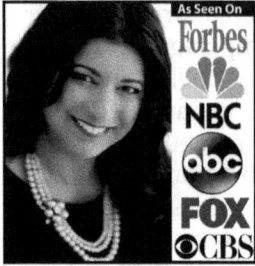

Moneeka Sawyer has often been described as one of the most joyful people you will ever meet. For over a decade she has been helping successful professionals, executives and entrepreneurs ease anxiety, overwhelm and stress so that they can experience more joy, ease and success in all areas of their lives.

She is the author of the international best-selling book, Choose Bliss: The Power and Practice of Joy and Contentment, which was recently honored with the very prestigious Woman of Impact Quill Award by *Focus on Women* magazine, the Quill Award for Best Literary Work from the governor of the state of Maryland, and the Pinnacle Book Achievement Award from the National Association of Book Entrepreneurs.

Moneeka, known as the blissful millionaire, was inducted into the Marquis Who's Who Biographical Registry, has been featured in *Forbes* magazine several times, is a TEDx speaker, hosts a highly acclaimed podcast and nationally syndicated radio show interviewing prestigious guests like Dr. Joe Vitale, Mark Victor Hansen and Leeza Gibbons. She has shared stages with Suzanne Sommers, Martha Stewart, and Ice T & Coco at places like the Nasdaq Marketplace, Harvard, and Carnegie Hall, and on TV on NBC, CBS, ABC, and Fox, reaching over 300 million people.

Email Address: **Moneeka@coreblisslife.com**
Website: **Blissfulinvestor.com**, **Coreblisslife.com**
Facebook page(s)
https://www.facebook.com/MoneekaSawyer
https://www.facebook.com/groups/blissfulinvestor/
https://www.facebook.com/BlissfulRealEstateInvestor/
https://www.facebook.com/coreblisslifeliveblissfromyourcore/
https://www.facebook.com/groups/alwayschoosebliss/
LinkedIn Page: **https://www.linkedin.com/in/moneeka-sawyer-4561145/**
YouTube Channel: **https://www.youtube.com/@moneekasawyer137**
Instagram: **https://www.instagram.com/moneekasawyer/**

Deborah Wiener is an international award-winning speaker. She is an entrepreneur, columnist for *RHG Digital Magazine*, international best-selling author and has been featured on numerous radio shows, podcasts and television shows. She is a distinguished Toastmaster.

Deborah has dedicated her life to being a catalyst for transformation, committed to guiding her clients towards empowerment, abundance and success. Through her innovative methodology, The Energetic Business Feng Shui System,™ she facilitates a profound journey of self-discovery, growth and inspiration. She illuminates your path to your unique purpose, shining a light on the door you were born to walk through.

Deborah is an active community leader and volunteer. She has served as an Arts for Oakland Kids board member. Deborah is available for speaking engagements and is a member of the Toastmasters Speakers Bureau.

Deborah Wiener is an expert who transforms challenges into solutions and dreams into reality by identifying what is blocking the energetic flow of money and success!

Email: **dwiener30@gmail.com**
Phone Number: 925-580-0350
Website: **http://www.deborahwiener.com**
Facebook: **https://www.facebook.com/deborah.l.wiener**
LinkedIn: **https://www.linkedin.com/in/deborah-wiener-b6009b167/**
Twitter: **@DeborahFengShui**
YouTube: **https://www.youtube.com/channel/UCean6OtIAhs44jLJy9v1izA**
Instagram: **https://www.instagram.com/fengshuibusinessconsultant/**

The Book Collective

This special collective came together to prepare messages to share with humans through the book project: *Wisdom From the Heart*. Each council or individual being or group of beings shared their messages with Rebecca, who in turn, translated and did her upmost to honor the vibration, energy and heartbeat of each message to share on their behalf with the readers of this book.

The Book Collective is made up of the following:

The Georgies, a one-and-a-half-year-old white and black, long-haired tuxedo cat that has multiple beings within her. They present themselves as The Georgies. We call her Georgie at home.

The Trees, a collective energy speaking from the trees' perspective.

Gaia is Mother Earth.

The Crystalline Council speak on behave of the crystalline encompassing/representing the energy of crystals.

The Animal Council, some call them the Animal Wisdom Council. This is a group representing and looking after Animals.

Twiggy is a stick bug that I met this past year. Twiggy is speaking from his heart/spirit to yours. Sharing his observations and wisdom with the humans who read this book.

They can be reached through Rebecca Hall Gruyter at **Rebecca@ YourPurposeDrivenPractice.com** or by slowing down and connecting with them from your heart.

CLOSING THOUGHTS

Dear Powerful Reader,

Thank you for reading our *Wisdom from the Heart* Daily Inspiration book. We hope it has touched your heart and spirit, encouraging and inspiring you!

I wanted to share a little bit more about our organizations, Your Purpose Driven Practice™ and RHG Media Productions.™ We are passionate about helping others live on purpose and with purpose in their life and business. I hope this book has supported and inspired you to choose to live on purpose and with great purpose!

If you are wanting to reach more people and be part of inspiring and supporting others with your message, your gifts and the work that you bring to the world, then I want to share some opportunities for you to consider.

Each year, we compile and produce anthology book projects, support authors in publishing their own powerful books as best sellers, produce and publish an international magazine. We would love to support you in reaching more people. Please take a moment to learn a little bit more about us at the sites listed below, and then reach out to us for a conversation. **We would love to have you join us as we seek to make a positive global difference.**

You can learn more about each of these things at our main website: www.YourPurposeDrivenPractice.com

Learn more about our **anthology writing opportunities**: www.YourPurposeDrivenPractice.com and click on the "anthology writing opportunities" button.

If you would like to connect with me personally to explore some of our opportunities in upcoming book projects, podcast/radio shows, here is the link to schedule a time to speak with me directly: www.MeetWithRebecca.com, or you can email me at Rebecca@YourPuposeDrivenPractice.com

May you always choose to step forward and SHINE!

Warmly,

Rebecca Hall Gruyter

Anthologies Compiled by Rebecca Hall Gruyter:

Anthologies Available Now Compiled by Rebecca Hall Gruyter:

SHINE Series
(compiled and led by Rebecca Hall Gruyter)

Come Out of Hiding and SHINE! (Book 1)

Bloom Where You Are Planted and SHINE! (Book 2)

Step Forward and SHINE! (Book 3)

Brilliance Series
(compiled and led by Rebecca Hall Gruyter)

Step Into Your Brilliance! (Book 1)

Step Into Your Brilliant Purpose! (Book 2)

Share Your Brilliance! (Book 3)

Experts and Influencers Series
(compiled and led by Rebecca Hall Gruyter)

Experts and Influencers Series: Leadership (Book 1)

Experts and Influencers Series: Women's Empowerment (Book 2)

Experts and Influencers Series: Step Forward With Purpose (Book 3)

Visibility Today!
(anthology compiled by Rebecca Hall Gruyter)

The Grandmother Legacies
(anthology compiled by Rebecca Hall Gruyter)

The Animal Legacies (anthology compiled by Rebecca Hall Gruyter)

Bloom & SHINE! (365 daily inspiration anthology compiled by Rebecca Hall Gruyter)

Empowering YOU, Transforming Lives (365 daily inspiration anthology compiled by Rebecca Hall Gruyter)

Wisdom from the Heart (365 daily inspiration anthology compiled by Rebecca Hall Gruyter)

Journals by Rebecca Hall Gruyter:

The Animal Legacies Journal

The Experts and Influencers Leadership Journal

The Experts and Influencers Women's Empowerment Journal

The Experts and Influencers Move Forward With Purpose Journal

Women's Empowerment Journal

Step Into Your Brilliance Journal

Step Into Your Brilliant Purpose Journal

Share Your Brilliance Journal

Wisdom From the Heart Journal

Books Featuring a Chapter by Rebecca Hall Gruyter:

The 40/40 Rules, anthology compiled by Holly Porter

Becoming Outrageously Successful, anthology compiled by Dr. Anita Jackson

Bright Spots, anthology compiled by Davis Creative

Catch Your Star, anthology published by THRIVE Publishing

Discover Your Destiny, anthology compiled by Denise Joy Thompson

Engaging Experts, anthology compiled by Davis Creative

I Am Beautiful, anthology compiled by Teresa Hawley-Howard

Movers & Shakers 2020, anthology compiled by Teresa Hawley-Howard

The Power of Our Voices, Sharing Our Story, anthology compiled by Teresa Hawley-Howard

Real Estate Investing for Women, anthology compiled by Moneeka Sawyer

Succeeding Against All Odds, anthology compiled by Sandra Yancey

Success Secrets for Today's Feminine Entrepreneurs, anthology compiled by Dr. Anita Jackson

The Unstoppable Woman of Purpose, anthology and workbook, compiled by Nella Chikwe

Women on a Mission, anthology compiled by Teresa Hawley-Howard

Women of Courage, Women of Destiny, anthology compiled by Dr. Anita Jackson

Women Warriors Who Make It Rock, anthology compiled by Nichole Peters

You Are Whole, Perfect, and Complete—Just as You Are, compiled by Carol Plummer and Susan Driscoll

www.ingramcontent.com/pod-product-compliance
Lightning Source LLC
Chambersburg PA
CBHW051709020426
42333CB00014B/900